BEER LOVER'S
COLORADO

Best Breweries, Brewpubs & Beer Bars

Second Edition

JOHN
FRANK

Globe
Pequot

Guilford, Connecticut

Globe Pequot

An imprint of The Rowman & Littlefield Publishing Group, Inc.
4501 Forbes Blvd., Ste. 200
Lanham, MD 20706
www.rowman.com

Distributed by NATIONAL BOOK NETWORK

British Library Cataloguing in Publication Information available

ISSN 2326-6805
ISBN 978-1-4930-4142-8 (paperback)
ISBN 978-1-4930-4143-5 (e-book)

∞™ The paper used in this publication meets the minimum requirements of American National Standard for Information Sciences—Permanence of Paper for Printed Library Materials, ANSI/NISO Z39.48-1992

Printed in the United States of America

NORTHWEST 139

ASPEN, BRECKENRIDGE, CARBONDALE, DILLON, EAGLE, FRISCO, GLENWOOD SPRINGS, GRAND JUNCTION, AND STEAMBOAT SPRINGS

SOUTHWEST 155

CORTEZ, DEL NORTE, DOLORES, DURANGO, GUNNISON, MONTROSE, OURAY, PAGOSA SPRINGS, RIDGWAY, AND TELLURIDE

BEER FESTIVALS 169

BEER STORES 179

BYOB: BREW YOUR OWN BEER 185

IN THE KITCHEN 199

PUB CRAWLS 213

APPENDIX

ACKNOWLEDGMENTS 234

INDEX 236

ABOUT THE AUTHOR & PHOTOGRAPHER 239

Not until you sit down with a list of all 350-plus Colorado breweries does the magnitude of the state's beer bona fides come into view. And not until you travel the entire state and visit as many of them as possible does a real appreciation for the beer scene become clear. This is how I started the book research. And despite spending years writing about Colorado beer, I didn't realize the true scope of the state's brewing landscape until now.

This book is intended for Colorado newcomers and craft beer beginners in the hope that it instills in both a deep appreciation of the state's breweries and culture. And it's written for the natives and longtime beer lovers in the hope that it continues to provide inspiration for exploration in the years to come. The bottom line, as I learned, is that there's something interesting and flavorful for everyone.

Colorado's modern beer story began four decades ago this year, when Boulder Beer Company became the first craft brewery in the state. The early days were not easy, as the pioneers know well, but they laid the foundation for something so much greater. Now, Colorado ranks as one of the top three states in the nation for the number of breweries and in the top five on a per capita basis, according to the Brewers Association, which is appropriately based in Boulder. The number of passionate beer ambassadors and talented brewers in Colorado is a testament to the state's brewing legacy. The stories on these pages highlight the state's beer history and spotlight the breweries that will define its future. And I hope the overall impression left behind is how much beer is intertwined with the Colorado brand.

So much has changed from 2012 when the first edition of *Beer Lover's Colorado* published. More than 200 breweries opened since then, and a significant number of others listed in the original closed. The first edition didn't include a handful of the well-regarded breweries that now carry the Colorado beer name across the nation, ones like WeldWerks Brewing Company, Black Project Spontaneous & Wild Ales, Casey Brewing & Blending, and TRVE Brewing. In Denver, the River North beer district didn't even exist, and Crooked Stave Artisan Beer Project was a mere glimmer at the time. Major Colorado breweries such as New Belgium, Odell, Great Divide, Breckenridge, and Oskar Blues had a much smaller footprint. To document all the growth in this book was an incredible journey, and now more than ever, Colorado deserves the title as the Napa Valley of Beer.

The challenge in writing a guidebook about Colorado beer is naming the best of the best in a state with so much good beer. And it's doubly hard because everyone's tastes are different—not to mention that new breweries are opening each week. Just about all beer lovers in Colorado can name their favorite brewery, and I hope I included as many as possible. But the reality is that this book includes a mere 25 percent of the state's breweries. A number of my favorite places didn't even make the cut.

To compile the list of breweries featured here, I visited them and dozens of others not listed. True to my journalistic training, I also referenced other rankings from reputable publications and consulted with a handful of Colorado beer experts to get a variety of opinions. (The experts are listed in the acknowledgments section.) My favorite part of the book research was tasting new and experimental beers from the source that highlight the brewers' creativity. In the end, the book features a variety of the best breweries in their respective regions, which is admittedly unfair for the beer-drenched Denver metro area and other Front Range cities where the competition is tough. The ones included in the book hit a number of highlights but overall made good beer and offered great service. I'm hopeful that the final list in the book offers a beer spot for everyone, whether you are a connoisseur or a novice, whether you like IPAs and sours or just a good lager. It's a privilege for me to tell the stories of these beer makers, but the words here offer just a glimpse of their dedication and passion. I encourage you to visit each, ask questions, and get to know the people who make the beer in your hand.

In the years ahead, the craft beer industry will continue to evolve and face significant challenges with a more competitive market and new alcohol laws in Colorado, both of which will change the business model and test the state's brewers. It's possible, if not likely, that one or more of the breweries or beer bars in these pages could unfortunately close. But based on my conversations with beer lovers from across the state whom I met as I researched this book, I'm confident that Colorado will continue to make great beer and great brands for us all to enjoy for many years to come. Because, after all, Colorado is "the state of craft beer."

Colorado is a well-recognized beer capital and brimming with too many breweries to list. This book does not try to document every single one. Instead, it is a guide to the most interesting and important breweries, brewpubs, bars, and festivals in each region of Colorado—the ones that are defining the state's beer landscape.

This guide is designed to be a fun resource for newcomers and craft beer connoisseurs in Colorado. The listings are organized alphabetically by geography. The brew-soaked regions of Denver, the Denver metropolitan area, Boulder, and Fort Collins are highlighted in their own sections. From there, the state is subdivided into four quadrants—northern Front Range, south-central, northwest and southwest—roughly split by the tall mountains of the Continental Divide that run north to south and an invisible line through the middle of the state.

The breweries listed in the book are a diverse lot—from international beer companies that call Colorado home to family-run, neighborhood brewers. The majority of them bottle or can their beer, and some even distribute widely across the state and nation. But the key to keep in mind is that the beer is always the freshest and best at the source. Each listing was current at the time of research, but double-check hours and details before visiting.

You can taste beer at all the breweries listed in the book. The breweries without public taprooms were not included, but you can look for them in the beer bars or the new beer stores section at the back of the book. The difference between the breweries and the brewpubs is more functional than academic in this guide. For the most part, the brewpubs in the book are places with a kitchen on premise that serves food, and in those listings, I identified a few menu items to whet your appetite. But keep in mind that most breweries allow outside food and often host food trucks on the curb if they don't serve themselves.

For each entry, I highlight the stories behind the place, people, and beers with a focus on what makes them rise above the crowd. The beers identified as flagships and seasonals, or listed in the narrative, are subject to change and certainly offer just a glimpse of the menu. A number of breweries are now eschewing the entire concept of flagship beers, and instead of keeping a handful of the same brews on tap at all times, they rarely, if ever, make the same one twice. My favorite part of a brewery visit is tasting new and experimental beers that don't make wider distribution and highlight the brewers' creativity. For selected breweries and brewpubs, a Beer Lover's Pick highlights a must-try showcase beer or a local's favorite, and I tried to offer a wide variety of styles.

A better appreciation for beer comes only from trying a range of styles, not just IPAs. The beer bars featured in the book offer this variety as well as hard-to-find beers that are best-in-class examples from Colorado and across the globe. I am admittedly biased toward exploration, finding new breweries and flavors on tap lists, so you'll see that reflected in the beer bar listings. Most of them also serve food, highlighting a growing recognition that pairing with beer makes for a more holistic tasting experience.

In addition to the brewery, brewpub, and beer bar listings in this guide, you'll also find chapters designed for locals and visitors alike:

Beer Festivals: A beer fest is a great way to try a variety of breweries or styles of beer. But not all festivals are made the same. Like other parts of the book, this section features the most interesting ones in the state—the ones that offer the best experience and best brews. These are the ones worth traveling to attend or paying the money to get inside. Keep in mind that the timing and formats are subject to change, so consult the hosts' websites for more details.

Beer Stores: Before 2019, only liquor stores in Colorado sold full-strength beer. But now, after a law change that abolished 3.2 beer, the real stuff is available in most grocery and convenience stores in addition to the liquor stores. The most discerning buyers, however, will visit a local bottle shop that employs a beer buyer and hand-selects its brews. This new section lists the places where you can find the best local and independent brewers, whether you want a six-pack for the football game or a special bottle to pack in a suitcase to take across the country.

BYOB: Brew Your Own Beer: This chapter is for the homebrewers who want to try their hand at re-creating some of the best beers available in Colorado. And there's nothing that gives you more respect for the professionals than realizing how hard it is to accurately clone a commercial beer. The recipes were generously provided by the respective breweries, and in some cases, this is the first time they've been published. In reading the recipes, some preexisting all-grain homebrewing knowledge is useful but certainly not necessary. All of them have been resized from their large commercial batches to a more manageable five-gallon batch. If you have questions, consult your local homebrew store for help.

In the Kitchen: The recipes in this section highlight food and drinks that feature beer as an ingredient or the perfect accompaniment. Some breweries, brewpubs, and beer bars in Colorado have kindly submitted recipes to re-create at home. If you don't have the exact beer from the recipe, you can substitute with a similar one in the same style.

Pub Crawls: Colorado's 300 days of sunshine a year are made for beer tours, whether walking or biking. The neighborhoods of Denver are the easiest place to map out a beer day, but it's not hard to link together breweries and beer bars in Golden, Colorado Springs, Durango, and other cities, too. This section highlights the areas with the highest concentration of beer places—including breweries not identified elsewhere in the book—and allows numerous options for customization. For more ambitious tours, look online for professional operators in the area.

ABV: The acronym stands for "alcohol by volume" and is known more commonly as the percentage of alcohol in a beer. A typical domestic beer is a little less than 5 percent ABV, but other beers, such as stouts, can reach well beyond 10 percent ABV.

Adjunct: An ingredient other than malt that is fermentable in the beer. Depending on the beer style, examples include oats, corn, syrups, honey, fruits, and vegetables. Other ingredients, such as coffee, spices, lactose, and chocolate, are often considered adjuncts but do not technically meet the definition.

Ale: A beer brewed with top fermenting yeast, making it different from a lager. Popular styles of ales include golden ales, pale ales, amber ales, stouts, and porters.

Barrel: The production of beer at a brewery is measured in barrels, which is equal to 31 gallons.

Barrel-aged: A type of beer that is aged in a wood barrel, a process that imparts flavors that distinguish it from the base style. The barrels used in brewing often held other liquids first, such as whiskey, bourbon, rum, cognac, gin, and tequila.

Bomber: A 22-ounce bottle of beer.

Brewery: A beer maker that sells the majority of its beer off-site but often has a taproom on premise.

Brewpub: A restaurant-brewery that sells a significant portion of its beer on-site.

Cask ale: Also known as real ales, cask ales are naturally carbonated and usually served with a hand pump rather than forced through a tap with carbon dioxide or nitrogen.

Clone beer: A clone beer is a homebrew recipe based on a commercial beer.

Craft beer: A small, independent, and licensed brewer, as defined by the Brewers Association, the industry's trade group. To qualify, a brewery must produce 6 million barrels of beer or less a year and retain at least 75 percent ownership within the craft industry.

Crowler: A 32-ounce aluminum can of beer, often filled on request, sold by breweries for off-premise consumption.

Dry-hopping: The practice of adding hops during or after the fermentation of a beer to boost the hop aroma in a finished beer.

Flagship: The core beers made by a brewery or brewpub that are typically available year-round and often packaged for distribution.

Foeders: Pronounced "food-er," these large wooden vats are used to age beer, typically sour beers.

Growler: A 64-ounce, or half-gallon, container of beer, typically glass, ceramic, or stainless steel, filled at breweries and brewpubs for off-premise consumption.

Hazy IPA: A style of IPA that is best known for its murky or turbid appearance and often exhibits a lower perceived bitterness than other examples of the style. It is also known as a juicy or New England–style IPA.

Hops: The flowers or cones of the plant *Humulus lupulus* that are used in beers to produce bitterness, flavor, and aroma, depending on when they are added in the brewing process.

IBU: The acronym for International Bittering Units. The scale is the traditional way to measure the bitterness of a beer, but studies are increasingly showing that it is an irrelevant mark.

IPA: The abbreviation for India Pale Ale, the most popular beer style in America. The name refers to the lore of using hops to preserve beer for shipment to East Asia.

Lager: A type of beer brewed with bottom-fermenting yeast, compared to the top-fermenting ale yeast. The beers are fermented at lower temperatures and take longer to produce. The popular examples include American lagers, black lagers, doppelbocks, Pilsners, and Vienna lagers.

Malt: Cereal grain that is steeped in water, germinated, and dried to provide fermentable sugars for the production of beer.

Mixed culture: A combination of different yeast and bacteria, whether *Brettanomyces*, lactobacillus, or pediococcus, used to ferment a beer and impart unique aromas and flavors.

Seasonal beers: A beer that is brewed only at a certain time of year to coincide typically with the seasons and then rotates out of production for a time.

Spontaneous fermentation: The process by which a beer is fermented by naturally occurring yeast and bacteria, typically by leaving the beer open to the air in a coolship.

Wort: The sweet liquid created from mashing grains and then boiling in a kettle to make beer. It is full of sugars that the yeast eat to convert into alcohol.

Yeast: The microorganisms added to beer at the fermentation stage to convert the sugars into alcohol.

Denver

Denver is one of the most celebrated beer capitals in America and the hub for Colorado's well-regarded beer culture. The city hosts the Great American Beer Festival each fall, drawing tens of thousands of beer lovers from across the country. And it is home to two national brands, Crooked Stave and Great Divide. The scene is so vibrant that out-of-town breweries are establishing outposts in the city to tap into a beer community with so much energy.

Denver's status as a landmark on the beer map began to emerge only since 2010 when the number of breweries and beer bars in the city increased 10-fold. The current number of breweries and brewpubs is a constantly moving target but stands north of 70 at the moment.

The maturity of the beer culture is a special quality. A new brewery can't open without establishing a niche, and it pushes the entire industry forward with each step. Most of the city's breweries offer something for everyone, but some specialize in certain beer styles, whether it's IPAs, sours, or stouts. The River North neighborhood, known as RiNo, has emerged as Denver's beer district with more than a dozen great breweries and even more beer bars and restaurants within walking distance of each other. The brewery taprooms are the best places to try the beer fresh and get a feel for the place.

BAERE BREWING COMPANY

320 Broadway, Unit E, Denver, CO 80203; (303) 733-3354; BaereBrewing.com
Founded: 2014 **Founders:** Kevin Greer and Ryan Skeels **Brewers:** Kevin Greer and Ryan Skeels **Flagship beers:** Saison, Strip Mall Pale Ale, C3(i)PA, Big Hoppy Brown, Baere-liner Weisse **Seasonal/special releases:** Table sour series, Reciprocity, Duplicitous, Bruin series, Four Grains series **Tours:** On request **Taproom hours:** Mon through Wed, 4 to 11 p.m.; Thurs, 2 to 10 p.m.; Fri and Sat, noon to 11 p.m.; Sun, noon to 8 p.m. Growlers, crowlers, and bottles to go.

Baere Brewing started like so many craft brewers. A couple homebrewers get together and decide to go pro and open their own brewery. Kevin Greer and Ryan Skeels started Baere with a small 2.5-barrel brew house and an obscure shop in a strip mall on Broadway, the main avenue leading south from downtown Denver. But the brewery continues to expand, and its focus on sour and barrel-aged beer is giving it a wider reputation.

The brewery's name is a reference to an Anglo-Saxon name for barley that is considered one of the inspirations for the word "beer." The tap list is constantly rotating and covers all the popular trends—from hazy IPA and gose

to barrel-aged stouts and beer slushies. It's a neighborhood place where the barrels are proudly displayed in the taproom and the bar is the most popular place to sit. About one-third of the brewery's beer is sour. The **Table Sour** series is a kettle sour refermented in stainless tanks with a mixed culture that allows the lactobacillus to establish a lemony character to the beer. Other sours are done in barrels, and the brewers let each develop their own character. The most popular item on the menu is the **C3(i)PA**. The flavor profile is a throwback to 2005 before IPA went crazy. The chinook, cascade, and centennial hops (hence the "C3" moniker) balance against a maltier base, making it a pretty classic American IPA.

BLACK PROJECT SPONTANEOUS & WILD ALES

1290 S. Broadway, Denver, CO 80210; (720) 900-5551; BlackProjectBeer.com
Founded: 2014 Founders: James Howat and Sarah Howat Brewers: James Howat, Skip Schwartz, and Alex Buck Flagship beers: Magic Lantern, Shadow Factory, Puzzle Palace Seasonals/special releases: Roswell, Stargate Tours: On request Taproom hours: Tues through Thurs, 4 to 10 p.m.; Fri and Sat, 2 to 11 p.m.; Sun, 2 to 8 p.m. Closed Monday. Limited bottles to go.

The mad scientist of the Colorado beer world is brewer James Howat at Black Project Spontaneous & Wild Ales. A microbiologist, Howat cultivated his own wild yeast before moving to all spontaneously fermented beers using a 12-barrel copper coolship. The brewery specializes in sours and wild ales inspired by Lambic styles from Belgium. Employing a centuries-old process, the wort is put in open-topped containers and exposed to the elements to collect natural yeasts and bacteria from the air. Once it's transferred to barrels or stainless-steel tanks, the captured microbes ferment the beer and add an element of terroir, or a local flavor, that makes the beer unique. Most Black Project beers are blended, and the average age of the finished product is about 18 to 20 months old. The process follows a certification that Howat helped develop to mark coolship beers made outside Belgium but in the same tradition called Methode Traditionnelle.

Black Project began as a side venture at Former Future Brewing Company, a neighborhood brewery known for its Salted Caramel Porter tucked between antique stores and marijuana shops on the main road south of downtown. In 2016, the Howats retired the Former Future brand to focus entirely on Black Project beers, and now the brewery serves only sours and wild ales, several of which won major awards. The brewery takes an aviation theme, and the bar is made from the wing of a plane.

Many of the beers on the taproom menu feature fruits like cranberry, guava, boysenberry, peaches, and cherries that add gorgeous tones and flavors to the funky sour base. Black Project bottles are hard to find, and releases often occur by lottery or draw long lines. The **Stargate** series, a favorite each fall, is a golden sour with fruit, often carbonated to higher levels to lend a sprightly,

Beer Lover's Pick

ROSWELL

Style: Lambic Inspired

ABV: 6 percent

Availability: Each summer in limited-release bottles

The Roswell series is a spontaneously fermented Lambic-inspired beer that features a handful of variants aged on different types of fruit—a lot of fruit. Brewer James Howat uses six pounds per gallon, right near the maximum that will fit into the vessel. The beers are aged for nine months in barrels. Unlike many sours, Roswell is low in acidity thanks to carefully selected barrels, and a barnyard funkiness flavor still manages to present itself through the rich fruit character.

tart flavor that blends well with the sweetness of fruit and the richness from the barrel.

CALL TO ARMS BREWING COMPANY

4526 Tennyson St., Denver, CO 80212; (720) 328-8258; CallToArmsBrewing.com

Founded: 2015 **Founders:** Chris Bell, Jesse Brookstein, and Jon Cross **Brewers:** Chris Bell and Jon Cross **Flagship beers:** The Ballroom Beer, CTA IPA, Oats and Hose, Shirtless Putin Catching Rays, Berkeley Tart Blonde **Seasonals/special releases:** More Like Bore-O-Phyll, Majestic Wolf Lamp, Costermonger, Beer Drinks You, Shirtless Putin Nuzzling with Dolphins **Tours:** On request **Taproom hours:** Mon through Thurs, 3 to 10 p.m.; Fri, 3 to 11 p.m.; Sat, noon to 11 p.m.; Sun, noon to 9 p.m. Growlers and crowlers to go.

Call to Arms Brewing is the neighborhood brewery that makes you want to live in the neighborhood. Located off Tennyson Street, a bustling row of local shops mixed with beer bars, restaurants, and a city park, the northwestern Denver brewery is low-key and inviting, drawing a mature crowd of locals and families. Inside, the warm, dark wood of the huge bar lends an English pub feel, accentuated by a couple leather couches that make for cozy seating and plenty of tables. Together, it creates a more memorable impression than other breweries located in warehouses and business parks.

Like so many Colorado breweries, Call to Arms was launched by brewers who cut their teeth at one of the state's major breweries. In this case, the three founders worked at Avery Brewing in Boulder and departed with a vision to do things differently. The beer menu is a mix of new and old styles with as many lagers as IPAs. In fact, the brewery tries to keep a lager on one of its 14 taps at all times, and it didn't produce a flagship IPA until more than a year after opening.

A local favorite, **The Ballroom Beer** is a domestic lager that will taste familiar, as it's a not-so-subtle remake of **Coors Banquet** and once went by the snarky name Khores. The brewery's taste for humor extends to its Shirtless Putin series—beers named after propaganda images of Russia's Vladimir Putin. The **Shirtless Putin Nuzzling with Dolphins**, a barrel-aged imperial Baltic porter with coffee, is a favorite, but you can more easily find on tap **Shirtless Putin Catchin' Rays**, a Czech dark lager. Call to Arms won top honors for its fresh hop **More Like Bore-O-Phyll** at the 2018 World Beer Cup.

CEREBRAL BREWING COMPANY

1477 Monroe St., Denver, CO 80206; (303) 927-7365;
CerebralBrewing.com
Founded: 2015 **Founders:** Sean Buchan, Chris Washenberger, and
Dan McGuire **Brewer:** Sean Buchan **Flagship beers:** Rare Trait,
Muscle Memory, Dark Galaxie **Seasonals/special releases:** Here Be
Monsters, Work From Home, Lens Flare, Bird of Paradise **Tours:** None
Taproom hours: Tues, 4 to 10 p.m.; Wed and Thurs, 2 to 10 p.m.; Fri
and Sat, noon to 11 p.m.; Sun, noon to 10 p.m. Closed Monday. Crowlers,
cans, and bottles to go.

Sean Buchan started making beer in his kitchen, and before long, with a few awards to his name, he went from hobbyist homebrewer to professional, putting aside a career as a physical therapist. (Buchan also loves photography and shot most the images for the first edition of this guidebook.)

From the start, the brewer and cofounder envisioned a neighborhood brewery, and he opened Cerebral in an old brick building just off Colfax Avenue, the city's gritty and colorful main street featured in Jack Kerouac's novel *On the Road* and once dubbed the "longest, wickedest street in America." Buchan made an early splash with hazy IPAs when few in Colorado were brewing the style, and his "house IPA," **Rare Trait**, remains a popular pick. Calibrate your tastes with the beer and then branch out with one of the other half-dozen beers

DREAMY THING

Style: Brett Saison
ABV: 6.9 percent
Availability: Off and on at the taproom

Cerebral brewer Sean Buchan loves collaborating with other breweries, and this beer is one made with Our Mutual Friend Brewing in Denver. The saison won a silver medal at GABF in 2016, and it features a house blend of *Brettanomyces* yeast that lends it a dry, funky flavor that dovetails with the citrus aroma from the dry hop with citra, centennial, and sterling hops. If it's not on the board, try Lens Flare or the Dimensions series saisons.

on the menu that experiment with hop combinations, often in collaboration with other big-name breweries.

The expanding list of barrel-aged offerings, from funky sour saisons to decadent adjunct stouts, is building more hype for Cerebral. But one of its newer ventures is barrel-aged lagers. What that means is the once-sparse taproom is now filled to the ceiling with barrels, most of which will become special-release beers months down the road. **Here Be Monsters**, a boozy bourbon barrel-aged imperial stout, and a similarly big breakfast porter called **Work From Home**, are sweet and decadent bottles worth sharing if you can get one. The brewery's saisons really showcase the brewery's maxim of science and art, as the name suggests. **Lens Flare**, a dry hoppy saison with simcoe, southern cross, and cascade hops, is a standout.

COMRADE BREWING COMPANY

7667 E. Iliff Ave., Unit F, Denver, CO 80231; (720) 748-0700; ComradeBrewing.com
Founded: 2014 **Founder:** David Lin **Brewers:** Marks Lanham and Mike Durland **Flagship beers:** Yellow Card Citra Blonde, REDCON, Koffee Kream Extra, Superpower **Seasonals/special releases:** Yellow Fever, Fresh Hop Superpower, Honeyman, Quit Stalin **Tours:** On request **Taproom hours:** Mon and Tues, 3 to 9 p.m.; Wed and

Thurs, noon to 10 p.m.; Fri and Sat, noon to 11 p.m.; Sun, noon to 9 p.m. Growlers and crowlers to go.

Comrade Brewing cemented its place as one of the state's best breweries with back-to-back GABF medals in a competitive category for its **Fresh Hop Superpower IPA**. The hop-forward theme extends to most its menu, whether the light touch in the **Yellow Card Citra Blonde** or the bold hops in the experimental IPA series **Honeyman**.

Owner David Lin and brewer Marks Lanham insist on making bright, clean beers and consider hazy IPAs a sign of poor technique. Lanham would know, as a much-decorated brewer who worked at Grand Teton Brewing, Boneyard

Beer Lover's Pick

SUPERPOWER

Style: IPA
ABV: 7.3 percent
Availability: Year-round and to go in growlers and crowlers
Superpower is a West Coast–style IPA that hits with big citrus and tropical notes in the aroma, a flavor that continues as you drink thanks to citra, simcoe, and mosaic hops. The bitterness is firm but balanced by the malt, a quality that is too often missed in today's outlandish IPAs. The dryness of the beer lets you order another and another until you wish it just flowed from a tap in your kitchen. The fresh-hopped version that debuts in late summer is even more pungent and delicious, and is a must-drink Colorado beer.

Beer, and Barley Brown's before he moved to Comrade. The brewery takes its name from the camaraderie that defined the early days of the craft beer industry and adopts a communist theme with a logo of hops, wheat, and yeast that looks like a Soviet sickle-and-hammer flag. A bright red wall is the first thing you see when you enter the spacious taproom with tall garage doors that open toward the parking lot, where a food truck is often parked.

Comrade is one of only a handful of breweries in the state with American-made brewing tanks and vessels, a point of pride. And its tap menu is unusual because it typically has a jalapeño beer, the best being the award-winning **Yellow Fever**.

COPPER KETTLE BREWING COMPANY

1338 S. Valentia St., #100, Denver, CO 80247; (720) 443-2522; copperkettledenver.com
Founded: 2011 **Founders:** Jeremy Gobien and Kristen Kozik
Brewers: Jeremy Gobien, Phil Natale, and Ryan Pollock **Flagship beers:** Mexican Chocolate Stout, Milk Stout, IPA, Citrus Paradisi, Bavarian Helles **Seasonals/special releases:** Moral Support DIPA, Charlie's Golden Strong, Menage a Quatre, Le Chapeau, Sobremesa, Snowed In series, Well Bred **Tours:** None **Taproom hours:** Mon through Tues, 2 to 9 p.m.; Wed through Thurs, 2 to 10 p.m.; Fri through Sat, noon to 10 p.m.; Sun, noon to 7 p.m. Cans, bottles, crowlers, and growlers to go.

Copper Kettle is the neighborhood brewery that packs a punch. North Carolina transplants Jeremy Gobien and his wife, Kristen Kozik, opened the brewery after years of homebrewing, with the mission of creating a neighborhood bar that welcomes friends and regulars.

The small taproom is located off the beaten path in a nondescript business park in southeastern Denver, but the brewery quickly established itself as a destination with its **Mexican Chocolate Stout**, which won GABF gold in its first year. It's a rich beer, yet not overpowering, and finishes with a dry heat kick.

The brewery is now known for a series of big beers. The **Snowed In** series starts as a barrel-aged imperial oatmeal stout and includes variants Coconut, Maple, and Mocha, the latter of which features chocolate and local coffee. All are great in those colder months. Likewise, the English-style barleywine **Well Bred** is aged in Breckenridge bourbon barrels and drinks boozy yet smooth at 10.7 percent. The beers—and a couple others—come in striking 19-ounce cans that are good fresh or cellared.

On the lighter side, and great on the brewery's patio in the sun, the **Bavarian Helles** is easy to drink and a solid representation of an overlooked style. Or try the **Citrus Paradisi**, an unfiltered IPA with big grapefruit flavor.

CROOKED STAVE ARTISAN BEER PROJECT

3350 Brighton Blvd., Denver CO 80216; (720) 550-8860; CrookedStave.com
216 N. College Ave., #130, Fort Collins, CO 80524
Founded: 2011 **Founder:** Chad Yakobson **Brewer:** Chad Yakobson
Flagship beers: Von Pilsner, IPA, St. Bretta, Colorado Wild Sage, Sour Rose, Petite sour series, Origin, L'Brett D'Or **Seasonals/special releases:** Coffee Baltic Porter, Trellis Buster, Do You Even Zest, Persica, Hop Savant, Nightmare on Brett, Surette Reserva, Mama Bear Sour Cherry Pie **Tours:** None **Taproom hours:** Sun through Tues, noon to 8 p.m.; Wed through Sat, noon to 10 p.m. Growlers, bottles, and cans to go.

Colorado native Chad Yakobson probably knows as much about the naturally occurring yeast *Brettanomyces* as anybody. His brewery, Crooked Stave, is an extension of his master's dissertation at Scotland's Heriot-Watt University.

Better known as Brett, the so-called wild yeast can add a range of flavors, whether mouth-puckering tartness, clean citrus notes, or funkiness that often is described as barnyard and dusty. Once a scourge blamed for ruining certain

wine and beer, Brett brewers like Yakobson actually highlight mixed-culture fermentation to create house blends of yeast and souring bacteria that develop signature flavors. The Brett beers at Crooked Stave take a refined approach, imparting citrus and tropical elements paired with dry earthy tones. Each is different. In the much-acclaimed **Nightmare on Brett**, the dark malts play with the yeast to create plum and chocolate cherry notes.

Beer Lover's Pick

PERSICA

Style: Golden Sour Ale
ABV: 6 percent
Availability: Limited release each June on tap and in bottles
Crooked Stave's Persica is one of the brewery's most coveted beers and gets released with great fanfare each June. Brewed with a mixed culture, it ages in huge oak barrels called foeders with organic Palisade peaches from Colorado's Western Slope. The fuzzy sweetness of the ripe peach is evident in the beer and blends well with the base beer, which features its own stone fruit flavors from the Brett yeast.

Crooked Stave Artisan Beer Project

Most of the best-known beers at the Denver taproom—located inside The Source, an indoor market and hotel—are sour but not all of them. An expansion at the Crooked Stave's off-site production brewery, which is not open to the public, made more room for top-flight beers like the juicy **IPA** and double IPA **Trellis Buster** as well as **Von Pilsner**, a keller pilsner that is thirst-quenching and crushable. Crooked Stave's push to experiment only continues with the addition of a new tasting room and small brew house in Fort Collins, where it originated in 2011.

DENVER BEER COMPANY/ CERVECERIA COLORADO

1695 Platte St., Denver, CO 80202 and 1693 Platte St., Denver, CO 80202; DenverBeerCo.com and CerveceriaColorado.com
5768 Olde Wadsworth Blvd., Arvada, CO 80002; (303) 433-2739
Founded: 2011 **Founders:** Charlie Berger and Patrick Crawford **Brewer:** Jason Buehler **Flagship beers:** Graham Cracker Porter, Princess YumYum, Incredible Pedal, Pretzel Assassin **Seasonals/ special releases:** Hey! Pumpkin, Big Juicy Freak Double IPA, Maui Express, Japance Off **Tours:** None **Taproom hours:** Mon through Thurs, 11 a.m. to 11 p.m.; Fri and Sat, 11 a.m. to midnight; Sun, 11 a.m. to 9 p.m., at both locations. Growlers and cans to go.

The sun shines about 300 days a year in Denver, and when it's warm, the communal beer benches at Denver Beer Company's downtown patio

are the place to be. Located just across a bridge over the Platte River from downtown, the brewery (a former auto shop) opens the large garage doors, plays music, hosts food trucks, and sports a youthful vibe reflective of the city at large.

Even if it's summer, you'll see people drinking their flagship **Graham Cracker Porter**, a gold medal beer. The **Princess Yum Yum Raspberry Kölsch** is a year-round favorite, too, while **Hey! Pumpkin** is a popular fall seasonal. But the beer chalkboard menu constantly changes, so you'll always find interesting new brews at the downtown location and the new outpost in Arvada, which features its own beers.

Next door to the Denver location is the brewery's colorful cousin, Cerveceria Colorado. Denver Beer Company's owners opened the Mexican-inspired brewery in 2018 in a barrel room space once reserved for special events. The Cerveceria beers, many of which started as collaborations with Mexican brewers, are innovative and bold in flavor, a refreshing new detour for your taste buds. Inside and out, the building features murals in bright reds, purples, and blues from two renowned local artists. Jason Buehler, who brews for both operations, drew inspiration for the beer from his travels through Mexico, where he worked with local brewers to design recipes that incorporate traditional flavors of cinnamon, chilies, nopal, mole, and lime, among others.

Beer Lover's Pick

GRAHAM CRACKER PORTER

Style: Porter
ABV: 5.9 percent
Availability: On tap and in cans year-round

This beer tastes like its name, and the original recipe actually calls for graham crackers. The first taste is all sweetness, but

Denver Beer Company

then the beer comes together with all the best elements of hearty American porter—milk chocolate flavor, espresso coffee notes, and a vanilla cookie aroma. It's a dessert beer to be sure but not so heavy that you can't have another. Look for variants throughout the winter.

The results include **Churro Stout** and **Poblano Pils** and many others on the rotating tap list. Get the **Venga**, a traditional Vienna lager, ordered chelada style with fresh lime juice and a salted rim.

FICTION BEER COMPANY

7101 E. Colfax Ave., Denver, CO 80220; (720) 456-7163; FictionBeer.com
Founded: 2014 **Founders:** Christa and Ryan Kilpatrick **Brewer:** Ryan Kilpatrick **Flagship beers:** Madame Psychosis, Logic Is Relative, Feely Effects, Malice and Darkness **Seasonals/special releases:** Alternate Present, Foreshadowing, HAL, Magic Wallet, A Wizard's Power, The Recurrence, Barrel Aged Malice and Darkness, Veritaserum, Wintry Emblem **Tours:** None **Taproom hours:** Mon through Thurs, 2 to 10 p.m.; Fri, 2 to 11 p.m.; Sat, 1 to 11 p.m.; Sun, 1 to 9 p.m. Growlers, cans, and bottled beers to go.

The bar is made of books. The beers are named for great characters or lines in literature. A tall bookshelf sits across the room from the bar. And the tap handles look like book spines. So whether you come to read and relax, drink a beer and relax, or both, Fiction Beer Company has you covered.

The brewery is located on the ground floor of an apartment building east of downtown on Colfax Avenue, which has inspired many a writer itself. The big windows and roll-up garage door keep it lighter than a dark, musty library and draw beer lovers and families alike to a large back patio.

Denver

New England–style IPAS are the main attraction at Fiction, but the brewery is expanding into sours, barrel-aged beers, and plenty of more traditional styles. Fiction took home one of the first GABF medals in the new hazy pale ale category for its **Madame Psychosis**. The beer is juicy in flavor but not overpowering and soft on the mouthfeel but not a milkshake. It presents flavors of mango, oranges, and peach. Other beers amplify the hops with double and quadruple dry-hopped versions. On the darker side, the **Malice and Darkness** stout appears in a series of barrel-aged editions and is a top pour for its rich flavors and big-barrel qualities.

GREAT DIVIDE BREWING COMPANY

2201 Arapahoe St., Denver, CO 80205
1812 35th St., Denver, CO 80216; (303) 296-9460;
GreatDivide.com
Founded: 1994 **Founder:** Brian Dunn **Brewer:** Brandon Jacobs
Flagship beers: Samurai Blonde Ale, Colette Farmhouse Ale, Strawberry Rhubarb Sour Ale, Denver Pale Ale, Titan IPA, HeyDay Modern IPA, Hercules Double IPA, Claymore Scotch Ale, Velvet Yeti Nitro Stout, Yeti Imperial Stout **Seasonals/special releases:** Orabelle Belgian-Style Tripel, Roadie Grapefruit Radler, Hoss Oktoberfest Lager, Hibernation English-Style Old Ale, Fresh Hop Pale Ale, Rumble Oak Aged IPA, Smores Yeti **Tours:** Both locations, Mon through Fri, 3 p.m., 4 p.m., 5 p.m.; Sat and Sun, 2 p.m., 3 p.m., 4 p.m., 5 p.m., 6 p.m. **Taproom hours:** Sun

through Tues, noon to 8 p.m.; Wed through Sat, noon to 10 p.m., at both locations. Growlers and bottled beers to go.

Great Divide is Denver's flagship brewery and the one most well-known outside the state, making its beers synonymous with the Mile High City. The company now operates in two locations in Denver—both with taprooms

Beer Lover's Pick

BARREL AGED YETI

Style: Barrel-Aged Imperial Stout
ABV: 12.5 percent
Availability: November to December
The limited-release, whiskey-aged beer is not as rare as the Yeti itself but is still quick to sellout. A sip captures the decadent flavors of bittersweet, alcohol-tinged, tiramisu dessert. Before it sees the light of day, this special version of Yeti spends at least 12 months conditioning in whiskey barrels. It is one of richer beers on the market in Colorado and goes well with dark months and snowstorms.

Great Divide Brewing Company

and tours—and remains a place for locals and tourists who value a diverse lineup of beers that deliver quality and not just hype.

Most of the beer production still takes place at the downtown brewery in the Ballpark neighborhood on Arapahoe Street, an easy walk from transit lines and hotels. But the new location in the RiNo neighborhood, off Brighton Boulevard, is the future. The massive red-sided warehouse sits on a five-acre property and houses the packaging facility as well as barrel-aged and sour beer storage. The future plans for the space include a larger brewery, beer garden, and restaurant. For now, you can visit the intimate Barrel Bar taproom, where oak staves line the walls and bar.

Both taprooms are the place to try beers you can't find outside Colorado and the standbys that made Great Divide a landmark. The brewery is best known for its enduring and ever-popular line of **Yeti** imperial stouts. In recent years, the Yeti brand has expanded well beyond its black-as-night, rich-chocolate, and heavily roasted malt-laden roots. **Chai Yeti** is a "spicy beast" and one of the newest additions to a roster that includes **Chocolate Oak Aged Yeti** and the pinnacle, **Barrel Aged Yeti**.

HOGSHEAD BREWERY

4460 W. 29th Ave., Denver, CO 80212; (303) 495-3105; Hogshead54.com
Founded: 2012 **Founders:** Jeff Kipp and Stephen Kirby **Brewers:** Stephen Kirby and Alex Bakken **Flagship beers:** Chin Wag, Gilpin Black Gold, Lake Lightning **Seasonals/special releases:** AK, Denver Pride, Boy's Bitter, Cook Lane, Downtown Julie, Hogshead Extra, Window Licker, Ye Old Burton Extra, Etta's, Finley's Farmhouse, Double Chin Wag, Barge's, Cross Channel Blonde, Divine Right, Lovibond **Tours:** None **Taproom hours:** Sun and Mon, noon to 10 p.m.; Tues and Wed, 2 to 10 p.m.; Thurs, noon to 10 p.m.; Fri and Sat, noon to 11 p.m.

The number of specialty brewers in Denver is a sign of the city's mature beer scene. Hogshead Brewery is one such place. Old-school English ales, served in a retrofitted old gas station, are what define Hogshead Brewery. The place takes a small neighborhood pub feel and specializes in cask-conditioned ales, poured through a hand pump from a cask that is kept at 50°F. The beer in the cask is unfinished, the brewers explain, and contains live yeast, which keeps the beer fresh through its entire life.

Hogshead is a temple for English beer fans, one of the best in its class. The **Chin Wag** is an Extra Special Bitter with a caramel malt sweetness that is delicately balanced with UK hops challenger golding and fuggles. Another traditional favorite is **Gilpin Black Gold**, a London porter. The beer is rich in

roasted malt, bitter chocolate, mustiness, and dark fruits and finishes with a soft mouthfeel from the cask conditioning. Not all the beers are served on cask, but when you visit a specialty brewer, it's worth taking their advice and getting one poured from the hand pump.

A fun trivia fact: Warner Bros. Entertainment once filed a legal challenge to block Hogshead Brewery's trademark. Why? It opened a Hog's Head Pub at the Wizarding World of Harry Potter amusement park at Universal Orlando Resort in Florida and tried to claim the rights to the name.

OUR MUTUAL FRIEND BREWING COMPANY

2810 Larimer St., Denver, CO 80205; (303) 296-3441; OMF beer.com
Founded: 2012 **Founders:** Andrew Brown, Andrew Strasburg, Bryan Leavelle, and Brandon Proff **Brewers:** Jan Chodkowski and Ryan Leavelle **Flagship beers:** Times Arrow IPA, Inner Light Pale Ale, Brown Ale, Novo Coffee Stout **Seasonals/special releases:** Weirding Way, Saison Trystero, Fixed Blade, Thanatoid **Taproom hours:** Mon through Thurs, 4 to 10 p.m.; Fri and Sat, noon to midnight; Sun, noon to 10 p.m. Growlers, crowlers, and bottles to go.

For anyone who calls beer their friend, this brewery knows how you feel. Our Mutual Friend's founders became acquainted through homebrewing, so when they opened a brewery, it seemed natural to dedicate it to their mutual friend, beer. The name, of course, also is the title of Charles Dickens's last

completed novel, and the brewery adopted a literary theme after it opened. A framed 100-year-old newsprint excerpt from the book sits above a fireplace, and behind the bar, a bookshelf holds an assortment of travel books and donated copies of *Our Mutual Friend*.

The brewery, better known as OMF, contributed to creating the city's beer hub when it opened in RiNo in 2012, and it keeps the local theme in its beers, which feature Colorado-grown malt and hops, in as many as possible. The lineup covers the spread from lagers and wheat ales to double IPAs and stouts. But their sours are winning the most acclaim with GABF medals three consecutive years—first for a barrel-aged sour and the next two for Brett beers. **Weirding Way** is an example of the focus on Brett beers. It's made with at least a dozen different strains and develops big tropical flavors without any actual fruit additions. **Trystero** is brewed with a single Brett strain and shows pineapple and grapefruit characteristics.

RATIO BEERWORKS

2920 Larimer St., Denver, CO 80205; (303) 997-8288; Ratio Beerworks.com
Founded: 2015 **Founders:** Jason zumBrunnen and Scott Kaplan
Brewers: Jason zumBrunnen, Colin Ford, and Mel Wilcox **Flagship beers:** Domestica, Dear You, Hold Steady, Antidote, Rented World, Repeater **Seasonals/special releases:** King of Carrot Flowers, Major Nights, New Wave, Stay Gold, Coffee Hold Steady, Genius Wizard
Taproom hours: Sun through Thurs, noon to 11 p.m.; Fri and Sat, noon to midnight. Growlers to go.

If Denver's beer district had a capital, it would be Ratio Beerworks on Larimer Street in RiNo. The brewery opened in 2015 and showcases the city's modern image with a hipster cool vibe and a youthful crowd that shares communal tables, plays yard games, and drinks craft beer.

The owners met in the punk scene in the late 1990s and went separate ways before joining forces to open the brewery in a cavernous space with open rafters that once held a distillery. Inside, the bar is lined with retro neon yellow bar stools, a photo booth sits in the corner, and the wall is patterned with a mid-century modern mural of colorful geometric shapes. The music theme is evident in the marquee sign that shows the beer list above the bar.

Outside, the patio features stadium seating, tables with umbrellas, and a backyard area for games illuminated by string lights at night. The colorful muraled wall, painted by artist Blaine Fontana, is a destination itself in the city's art scene and features a portrait of Louis Pasteur, the French microbiologist who invented pasteurization and fermentation, as well as a pictorial narrative that describes Ratio's story.

The beer list is traditional with a modern twist, highlighting traditional styles reinvented with American creativity. A perfect example is the fan favorite **Dear You**, a dry and slightly tart French saison that is brewed and dry-hopped with

Beer Lover's Pick

GENIUS WIZARD
Style: Whiskey Barrel–Aged Russian Imperial Stout
ABV: 12.5 percent
Availability: December through February

Ratio is expanding its offering of barrel-aged beers, but its trademark Genius Wizard is one to seek out. The rich chocolate and molasses notes from the stout and the tobacco and leather tints from the oak barrels make for a complex combination. It's a big beer that can age for a couple years. And look for small-batch variants with different flavors at special events in the winter months.

Ratio Beerworks

Citra for an aroma resembling an IPA. The **Repeater** is an extra pale ale made with roasty malts, making it different than most in the category. And the **Hold Steady** is a chocolate rye Scotch ale that is uncommonly sessionable despite its dark appearance and big flavor.

RIVER NORTH BREWERY

6021 Washington St., Unit A, Denver, CO 80216; (303) 296-2617; RiverNorthBrewery.com
3400 Blake St., Denver, CO 80205
Founded: 2012 **Founders:** Matt and Jessica Hess **Brewer:** Matt Hess **Flagship beers:** Colorado IPA, Mountain Haze, River North White, Pils, FarmHouse, Tripel, J. Marie, Quandary, Mr. Sandman **Seasonals/special releases:** Barrel Aged Mr. Sandman, Nightmare Fuel, Whiskey Barrel Quandary, Whiskey Barrel J. Marie, Barrel Aged Avarice, The Decennial Series, Barrel Aged Nightmare Fuel, Barrel Blonde, Corundum **Tours:** None **Taproom hours:** Wed through Fri, 4 to 9 p.m.; Sat, noon to 9 p.m.; Sun, noon to 7 p.m. Crowlers, cans, and bottles to go.

River North Brewery took its name from the neighborhood where it was located—before the neighborhood even became the city's beer hub. But then it was forced to move when the building owner tore it down and built an apartment complex. River North moved way north to a production facility and small taproom on Washington Street. But it recently returned to its home turf with a second brewery on Blake Street and an additional brew system that cranks out smaller batches of beer.

The Washington Street location features 12 to 16 taps and sells beer to go in racing-stripe cans and bottles. **Mr. Sandman** is probably the brewery's best-known beer after it placed first in a national magazine's blind tasting. It's pure stout with a big roasted flavor and none of the adjunct ingredients that seem to define the category these days. A Belgian-style imperial stout aged in whiskey barrels, **Barrel Aged Avarice**, is another rare find and top brew.

The lineup includes six-packs of a farmhouse white, hazy IPA and pilsner. But locals return to the original Belgian styles that defined the early days, like the **J. Marie**, an imperial saison named for the brewer's wife that is nuanced and flavorful, a classic River North beer.

STATION 26 BREWING COMPANY

7045 E. 38th St., Denver, CO 80207; (303) 333-1825; Station26Brewing.com
Founded: 2013 **Founder:** Justin Baccary **Brewers:** Wayne Waananen and Allen Anderson **Flagship beers:** 303 Lager, Tangerine Cream, American Copper, Juicy Banger IPA, Bang Bang Double IPA **Seasonals/ special releases:** Birthday Beer, Fresh Hop Juicy Banger, Oktoberfest Lager, Milkshake IPA, Bourbon Barrel Aged Imperial Stout **Tours:** None **Taproom hours:** Mon through Sat, 1 to 11 p.m.; Sun, 1 to 9 p.m. Growlers and crowlers to go.

Housed in a renovated old fire station that gave the brewery its name, Station 26 anchors the east side of Denver. Its proximity to Denver International Airport makes it a common early stop for beer tourists, and whether visitors or locals, the tap list is often rotating with interesting seasonals for everyone in addition to the standbys. The brewery bought a food truck that is parked onsite called Order 26, and the taproom is particularly busy for special events, like a once-a-month Sunday bluegrass brunch and a Black Friday beer release.

Station 26 fancies its beers as classic to style and approachable for a large swath of beer drinkers, a philosophy that breaks from others who chase trends

Beer Lover's Pick

TANGERINE CREAM

Style: Cream Ale
ABV: 5.2 percent
Availability: Year-round on tap and in cans
Tangerine Cream is a conversation starter on the patio at Station 26, often drawing polarizing viewpoints. For some, the addition of tangerine and vanilla beans to the lager base tastes like the creamsicle from the neighborhood ice cream truck, the very definition of summer. To others, it's a little sweet and only drinkable in smaller quantities. Regardless of what you think, it's an interesting sip.

and get weird. But it also features new beers like milkshake IPAs at times. The brewery's most popular beer is **Juicy Banger IPA**. West Coast in style, the beer is made with Colorado craft malt and packed with tropical fruit flavors like papaya and more IBUs than you can count. The second most popular is **Tangerine Cream**, which the brewery calls "sunshine in a glass." Each fall, the brewery releases a Russian imperial stout and a barrel-aged version with different iterations from blueberry to a Manhattan cocktail edition that draw crowds.

TRVE BREWING COMPANY

227 Broadway, #101, Denver, CO 80203; (303) 351-1021; TrveBrewing.com
Founded: 2012 **Founder:** Nick Nunns **Brewer:** Zach Coleman
Flagship beers: Cosmic Crypt, Seven Doors, Score, Decreation, Stout O))), Cursed, Duried Sun, Ancient Bole **Seasonals/special releases:** Exhumation, Esprit de Corpse, Suffering Soul, Red Chaos, Life's Trade
Tours: None **Taproom hours:** Mon through Thurs, 3 to 11 p.m.; Fri through Sat, noon to midnight; Sun, noon to 10 p.m. Crowlers, bottles, and cans to go.

Take one step inside TRVE Brewing, and you'll realize this is not your typical craft brewery. It's dark, and heavy metal music, incomprehensive to all but the closest fans, is blaring from the speakers. A long Viking table at the front leads to the bar in the back, where beards and black T-shirts drink counterculture sours and IPAs. TRVE's brewer once said the beer was informed

by "absurdity and rebellion." In other words, the brewery is dedicated to not following style guidelines and doing everything differently.

The name (pronounced "true") references a term for uber-metal fans, and the music theme pervades the brewery, including the logos designed by an album artist with plenty of pentagrams, skulls, and skeletons. The loud image belies the nuanced beers on the menu, which ranges from hazy IPAs to spontaneously fermented sours. The mixed-culture sours and farmhouse pale ales form the core of a beer list that began on a nanobrewery system but later expanded to a second location, a production facility dubbed the "Acid Temple." TRVE's rapid rise is evident in the popularity for certain bottle releases and a long list of major breweries that have collaborated with them. **Cosmic Crypt** is the easy-drinking farmhouse pale ale, and **Cursed** is a mixed-culture sour pale ale that is tart and bright.

BIERSTADT LAGERHAUS

2875 Blake St., Denver, CO 80205; (720) 570-7824;
BierstadtLager.com
Founded: 2016 **Founders:** Bill Eye, Ashleigh Carter, and Chris Rippe
Brewers: Bill Eye and Ashleigh Carter **Flagship beers:** Slow Pour Pils,
Helles, Dunkel **Seasonals/special releases:** Vienna Lager, Maibock,
Doppelbock, Marzen **Tours:** On request **Taproom hours:** Sun through
Thurs, 11 a.m. to 10 p.m.; Fri and Sat, 11 a.m. to midnight. Growlers and
crowlers to go.

Bierstadt Lagerhaus specializes in what you could lovingly call beer-flavored
beer. Bill Eye and Ashleigh Carter, the founders and brewers, describe it
this way: "No flair, no twist, no added things. Just tradition." In other words: no
IPAs, no fruited brews. Just crisp, clean German-style lagers.

The dedication to the Old World makes Bierstadt stand out from the crowd
in a state that pushes the limits on beer. Eye and Carter, a dynamic duo with a
long brewing history, use a German copper kettle that is nearly a century old
at their operation inside the Rackhouse Pub in Denver's RiNo neighborhood.
The beers adhere to the ancient *Reinheitsgebot*, or beer purity law, that limits

Beer Lover's Pick

SLOW POUR PILS

Style: Northern German Pilsner
ABV: 5.1 percent
Availability: Year-round on tap and to go in growlers and crowlers

The time it takes to pour this beer gives you the opportunity to appreciate how difficult it is to make so well. The pale lager is pure art in the glass. Bierstadt's Bill Eye and Ashleigh Carter spent years working on the craft and specialized in the style. It's a brewer's favorite—the crisp, refreshing malt-forward beer you reach for at the end of a shift because you can drink more than one. Once you try it at the brewpub, you'll order another, too.

---

ingredients to barley, hops, and water. But don't let the simplicity suggest a lack of sophistication. It actually requires perfection.

The **Slow Pour Pils**, which is considered by some as the best beer in the state, takes 27 to 30 hours to brew and then lagers inside the tank for 10 weeks. At the bar, you'll need to wait another three to five minutes while it pours with a white foam head that rises above the rim of a tall, slender glass like 14,000-foot Mount Bierstadt over the horizon just to the West.

Each beer is poured into its respective glass, whether at the brewery or at a limited number of bars and restaurants in the city with enough dedication to pour Bierstadt's lagers. The **Helles** fills a half-liter mug built for toasting and drinking at 5 percent ABV. The brewery's third year-round beer is a **Dunkel**. It pours a dark mahogany color with rich bread flavors and even hints of chocolate. (In German, Helles means "light" and Dunkel means "dark.") The brewpub is located in a big brewing warehouse and shares space with a cidery. Rackhouse is the food side, and it offers a menu of traditional fare.

BLUE MOON BREWING COMPANY

3750 Chestnut Place, Denver, CO 80216; (303) 728-2337; BlueMoonBrewingCompany.com
Founded: 1995 **Founder:** Keith Villa **Brewers:** John Legnard and Ben Knutson **Flagship beers:** Blue Moon Belgian White Ale, Mango Wheat, Blood Orange Pale Ale, Iced Coffee Blonde **Seasonals/**

special releases: Lemondrop Pilsner, Summer Honey Wheat, Harvest Pumpkin, Spiced Belgian Abbey, Peach/Plum Noir, Winter Wheat, Mexican Chocolate Stout **Tours:** Self-guided **Taproom hours:** Sun through Thurs, 11 a.m. to 9 p.m.; Fri and Sat, 11 a.m. to 10 p.m. Growlers to go.

The ubiquitous **Blue Moon Belgian White** was first brewed in 1995 by Coors brewer Keith Villa, who wanted to make something different at the Sandlot Brewery located at Coors Field, home of the Colorado Rockies baseball team. The birthplace explains the beer's original name of Bellyslide Belgian Wit before it took another from the phrase "once in a blue moon," a reference to its rarity at the time. Now, the beer is so popular that it birthed its own stand-alone brewery in Denver, a short drive from the home of its parent company Coors in Golden.

In 2016, Blue Moon Brewery opened in RiNo as a stunning monument to beer with a self-guided tour, shimmering tanks visible through glass windows, a circular bar filled with glassware, and booths arranged inside sections of massive concrete pipeline. The brewpub features more than 20 rotating taps, along with an elevated food menu, and serves as a laboratory to test new beers for the national brand. The expansion allowed the Sandlot Brewery, still located in the stadium downtown, to return to its roots of brewing award-winning German lagers.

Even though Blue Moon is not counted as a craft brewer because of its owner, it maintains the same spirit of creativity, offering beers with a wide range of flavors, from the citrusy **Orange Blossom Kölsch** to **Blackberry Honey Barleywine**. And yes, you can still order a **Blue Moon Belgian White Ale**.

Beer Lover's Pick

BLUE MOON BELGIAN WHITE ALE

Style: Belgian Witbier
ABV: 5.4 percent
Availability: Year-round on tap and in bottles and cans

For many, Blue Moon became the gateway beer to the wider world of craft brew. And for many others, it remains a go-to beer. The birth of the beer is storied and an important part of brewing history in Colorado. The hazy, soft-white, effervescent ale strays from the traditional Belgian model only with a little more sweetness, delivering a vibrant citrus aroma and flavor. And trying one from the source is pretty much a bucket list item.

Denver

BULL & BUSH PUB & BREWERY

4700 Cherry Creek South Dr., Denver, CO 80246; (303) 759-0333; BullandBush.com
Founded: 1997 **Founders:** Dale Peterson and Dean Peterson
Brewers: Gabe Moline and Josh Bisk **Flagship beers:** Big Ben Brown Ale, MAN BEER, The Tower E.S.B. **Seasonals/special releases:** Happy Hop Pilsner, Allgood Amber Ale, Royal Oil, Legend of the Liquid Brain, Ghoul Fuel, Yule Fuel **Tours:** None **Taproom hours:** Mon through Fri, 11 to 2 a.m.; Sat and Sun, 10 to 2 a.m. Food service until midnight each night. Growlers, crowlers, and bottles to go.

Bull & Bush is a Denver beer institution. The British-style pub, full of dark wood and TV screens showing local sports, opened in 1971 and was modeled off another bar by the same name outside London. The adjacent brewery made its first beer back on New Year's Day in 1997. The pub now pours more than a dozen beers, with a handful of year-round offerings and many seasonals, along with a couple dozen guest taps. The pub also maintains a good-size bottle list. If whiskey is preferred, Bull & Bush has that covered with a well-stocked list of more than 200 choices.

The core beers are skewed mostly toward traditional English styles. The **Tower E.S.B.** is one of the finest examples. This beautifully balanced and award-winning beer is definitely an easy-drinking lighter option. Another decorated flagship is the **Big Ben Brown Ale**, a pretty garnet-colored classic

designed for pint-after-pint enjoyment. The aroma is rich with black treacle, toffee, and caramel. The drink has layers of dried dark fruit and roasted mixed-nut flavor. The annual tapping of the pub's 11.5 percent ABV bourbon barrel-aged imperial stout, **Legend of the Liquid Brain**, is always a popular event. The beer is something of a local legend among Colorado beer geeks, a sticky sweet chocolate malt bomb with brilliant notes of toffee and vanilla.

The food at Bull & Bush is above par and can best be described as Colorado meets British. Alongside the requisite fish-and-chips, you'll find popular and long-standing house staples like green chili and mashed potatoes.

GRATEFUL GNOME SANDWICH SHOPPE AND BREWERY

4369 Stuart St., Denver, CO 80212; (720) 598-6863; The GratefulGnome.com
Founded: 2018 **Founder:** Dan Appell **Brewer:** Bess Dougherty
Flagship beers: Giggity IPA, Brown Ale, Blond Ale, Session Stout, Pale Ale **Seasonals/special releases:** Imperial Red IPA, Dunkel Weiss, Tangerine Wheat **Tours:** None **Taproom hours:** Mon through Fri, 11 a.m. to 11 p.m.; Sat through Sun, 10 a.m. to 11 p.m. Kitchen closes an hour earlier.

It's safe to say that Bess Dougherty is beyond grateful that her new venture is open. Just weeks before the Grateful Gnome Sandwich Shoppe and Brewery's anticipated debut in 2017, construction scaffolding from an apartment building next door collapsed, damaging the brewery's roof and delaying the opening by months. Dougherty, the head brewer, was at the bar when it happened, and a plank that crashed through the brewery's ceiling missed her by just feet.

The delays and setbacks aside, the East Coast–styled deli opened in early 2018, and Dougherty, who previously worked at Wynkoop Brewing, is now making beer on her own system in her own style. Instead of crazy cult beers, Dougherty is a throwback. She says simple is better, and she makes beers to style. The **Grateful Gnome Brown Ale** and the **GnomeSpot Dunkel Weiss** will remind you why traditional styles are the reason you started drinking craft beer.

Most of the beers are sessionable with low alcohol content and pair well with the 50 sandwich offerings imagined by Dan Appell, whose father owned a sandwich shop in New Jersey where he worked from an early age. The meat is sliced at the counter inside the cozy building with exposed brick walls. Appell imagines it as the kind of place you can eat lunch seven days a week—a challenge that sounds worth accepting.

LIBERATI OSTERIA & OENOBEERS

2403 Champa St., Denver, CO 80205; (303) 862-5652; liberatidenver.com

Founded: 2018 **Founder:** Alex Liberati **Brewers:** Alex Liberati and Bob Malone **Flagship beers:** Parvus Titan, Facta Non Verba, Lupulus Vinifera, In Medio Stat Virtus, Dictum Factum **Seasonals/special releases:** Nomen Omen, Recioto Denveris, I-3PO, Oximonstrum **Tours:** None **Taproom hours:** Mon through Thurs, 4 to 10 p.m.; Fri through Sun, noon to 10 p.m. Bottles to go.

Call them Italian Grape Ales (IGAs) or wine-beer hybrids; either way, these Liberati brews are probably unlike anything you've ever tasted. Brewer Alex Liberati, a native of Rome, calls them oenobeers, from the Latin word for wine. The brews are produced with grapes, whether must, juice, or pomace. The wine element makes up to 49 percent of the fermentables, making some just barely beer. The acids from the grapes add a different twist, but the menu features traditional styles.

These beers offer an example of how it works: The **Lupulus Vinifera IPA** is made with 20 percent Pinot Grigio grapes. The **In Medio Stat Virtus**, a Belgian golden ale, contains a 48 percent addition of Chardonnay grapes. And the **Dictum Factum** stout features 25 percent Cabernet Sauvignon grapes. In each case, the wine flavors blend with the hops and grain to offer a different take on a traditional style.

The oenobeers are a complement to the osteria, or the restaurant, side of Liberati. The menu is traditional Italian from bruschetta to ravioli, presented beautifully on the plate, and the staff will help pair meals with a beer. The venue is simple yet bright, with lights reflecting off the steel brewing tanks. The uniqueness of the beers, and the beautiful setting, makes Liberati a place to stop, even if the wine-beer hybrids are not for everyone.

WYNKOOP BREWING COMPANY

1634 18th St., Denver, CO 80202; (303) 297-2700; Wynkoop .com

Founded: 1988 **Founders:** John Hickenlooper, Jerry Williams, Mark Schiffler, and Russell Schehrer **Brewers:** John Sims, Jay Lima, and Charles McManus **Flagship beers:** Rail Yard Ale, Mile High Pale Ale, Monk-y Business, Colorojo Red Ale, Light Rail Ale, B3K Black Lager, Belgorado IPA, Cowtown Milk Stout, Wixa Weiss, Uber Lager, Patty's Chili Beer **Seasonals/special releases:** Rocky Mountain Oyster Stout, Nug Life IPA, LoDo IPA. **Tours:** Tues through Sun, 2 p.m. and 3 p.m. **Taproom hours:** Sun through Thurs, 11 a.m. to midnight; Fri and Sat, 11 to 2 a.m. Growlers and crowlers to go.

Wynkoop Brewing Company opened a brewpub and billiards hall in 1988 in the century-old J. S. Brown Mercantile Building, a downtown

warehouse in a dilapidated Denver neighborhood. Defying expectations, Wynkoop, the first brewpub in Colorado, became a success and a catalyst for a decades-long downtown revival. The city's jewel (Union Station) sits across the street, Coors Field is blocks away, and construction cranes continue reshaping the skyline each day. So it's no exaggeration when Wynkoop says its beer built a neighborhood. One of its founders, John Hickenlooper, even went on to become Denver's mayor and Colorado's governor.

The house menu is much loved by Denver locals and out-of-town regulars alike. The standard brewpub fare with elevated offerings, like a short rib grilled cheese, appear alongside fresh and healthy options that fit the Colorado lifestyle. In addition to more than 10 house beers, Wynkoop is constantly pushing the envelope, following the legacy of the original brewer, Russell Schehrer. The **Rocky Mountain Oyster Stout** is the prime example. Made with roasted bull testicles (the mountain's oysters), the beer started as an April Fool's joke but now is an annual release that thankfully tastes nothing like a bull's anything.

The brewery is making barrel-aged and sour offerings to keep on the trendy edge, but mainstays, like its spicy **Patty's Chili Beer** and its bitter yet balanced **Mile High-P.A**, remain on the menu of more than two dozen beers.

Beer Lover's Pick

ROCKY MOUNTAIN OYSTER STOUT

Style: Foreign Export Stout
ABV: 7.2 percent
Availability: Limited release but regularly available

The Rocky Mountain Oyster Stout is the joke heard around the world. Once an April Fool's Day prank created by former brewer Andy Brown, it's now one of the most requested beers, and the brewers work hard to keep it on year-round. It starts by grilling bull's testicles, the oysters of the mountains, with three balls per barrel of beer, roasted until they are charred. Each weigh about one pound. The beer itself is roasted and full-bodied with a dark brown head. The testicles lend little if any flavor, for better or worse.

Wynkoop Brewing Company

THE CRAFTY FOX TAPHOUSE AND PIZZERIA

3901 Fox St., Denver, CO 80216; (303) 455-9666; craftyfox
.beer
Taps: 60 **Bottles/cans:** 30+

Located on Fox Street across the interstate northwest of downtown, Crafty Fox Taphouse and Pizzeria boasts 60 taps. The owner, Kyle Moyer, suggests it's "the minimum selection" needed to offer a roster of great craft beer. And he would know. Moyer also owns Bogey's Beer and Wine, the specialty liquor store next door that hunts for rare and unique beers to stock the shelves.

The beer list often includes the likes of WeldWerks, Beachwood, and Perennial breweries. The menu is designed for sampling with five-ounce drafts for most beers in addition to full pours. And the dedication extends to the food, where menu items are made with ingredients from local breweries and designed to pair with certain beer styles. The menu includes salads and specialty pizzas, as well as sandwiches and beer-drinking favorite appetizers like chicken wings.

Grab a beer and a bite at the expansive square-shaped bar on the main floor, near huge windows that open when the weather is nice. Or if it's open, take a pint upstairs to the second-floor deck, which offers views of a city skyline that lights up at dusk when the sun sets behind the mountains.

EUCLID HALL BAR & KITCHEN

1317 14th St., Denver, CO 80202; (303) 534-4255; EuclidHall
.com
Taps: 19 **Bottles/cans:** 100

Founded by Jennifer Jasinski and Beth Gruitch, the much-lauded owners of four nearby high-end restaurants, Euclid Hall Bar & Kitchen takes the concept of good beer and good food to haute cuisine levels. Located just around the corner from Denver's historic and picturesque Larimer Square, Euclid pairs its outstanding menu with a dozen seasonal taps and seven rotating beers that are primarily local craft beer but include a handful of top-in-class breweries from outside Colorado. A cleverly subdivided bottle and can beer menu arranges offerings in increasing levels of boldness and complexity. The first category is "Arithmetic," which is followed by "Algebra," "Geometry," "Trigonometry," "Calculus," and "Quantum Mathematics." A cellar list offers even more with top-dollar, limited-release beers, often in bigger 750-milliliter or 22-ounce formats.

From the start, the appetizers signal you're not at a run-of-the-mill beer bar. Try pad Thai pig ears, brûléed center-cut beef marrow bones, fried cheddar curds, and more. A selection of Montreal-inspired poutines—plates of hand-cut french fries covered in melted cheese curds and gravy—are the favorites. The entrees vary with new chef specials that build on favorites like the chicken and waffles and Pabst Blue Ribbon mussels. A highlight on the menu for the beer-drinking crowd is fresh hand-cranked sausages from around the world and a selection of mustards.

FALLING ROCK TAP HOUSE

1919 Blake St., Denver, CO 80202; (303) 293-8338;
FallingRockTapHouse.com
Taps: 75+ Bottles/cans: 130+

Falling Rock Tap House is a Denver beer institution. The bar is known far and wide as the place to drink beer in Colorado. And owner Chris Black is a legend in his own right as an outspoken evangelist for craft beer. The bar's motto: "No crap on tap."

Just down from Coors Field, the place is busy all summer. But in the fall, when GABF takes over Denver, Falling Rock hits its stride as the unofficial hub for the best beers, brewers, and rabble-rousing. The more than 75 taps that Falling Rock pours year-round are always interesting and often feature very limited beers. Black prides himself on being able to source some of the rarest bottles and kegs in the world.

One regular tap is Russian River's **Pliny the Elder**, the standard-setting IPA from California that is tough to find outside the brewery. The newest and most rare beers appear on a special board way up top, behind the bar, and it rotates constantly. Order by number. The paper menus list dozens more options, and it's so dense that it takes multiple reads to realize all the beers available. If—for some crazy reason—you can't find what you want on tap, turn to the 130-plus bottles in the cooler. The food—basic bar fare of burgers, chicken tenders, and wings—is not the main attraction. It's the beer.

FINN'S MANOR

2927 Larimer St., Denver, CO 80205; FinnsManor.com
Taps: 16 Bottles/cans: 12+

The eclectic Finn's Manor is first and foremost a cocktail bar. It specializes in whiskeys, numbering at more than 160. The rare and expensive bottles sit next to gins, tequilas, mezcals, rums, and liqueurs on floating shelves extending from the ceiling. The bartenders will mix and create, offering a few special cocktails that always seem to fit the season and mood. Second, Finn's Manor is a food truck bazaar. The vintage exposed-brick bar, with Spanish moss hanging from the ceiling, gives way to an area with outdoor seating and an open-air courtyard where half a dozen trucks, rotating regularly, park under an awning.

The beer, however, is the secret. The 16-tap menu at Finn's Manor is possibly the most artfully curated in the city. The constantly rotating list spotlights a handful of the best local brews and some of the most unique from across the US and the world. The place's reputation for beer is getting noticed, increasingly drawing tap takeovers and vintage brews from elite breweries. It's a great place to let your palate go in new directions with good food trucks and special beers, all the while placating friends who prefer a stiff liquor drink. And don't miss the beer shed out back with even more rare beer bottles and cans.

FIRST DRAFT TAPROOM & KITCHEN

1309 26th St., Denver, CO 80205; (303) 736-8400;
FirstDraftDenver.com
Taps: 40 Bottles/cans: 40+

Let's face it: Colorado's beer scene is so robust that it's hard to cover all the territory in a year, let alone a weekend. And even if you visit a handful of breweries, you still can't taste everything on their menus. So a place that offers 40 taps, many of them local beers, and gives you the ability to pour as much or as little as you want, is a good stop.

Consider First Draft Taproom & Kitchen a crash course in beer geography and style. The RiNo neighborhood bar gives you a card to swipe on a lengthy tap wall with a full range of beers. My favorite exercise is grabbing two or three glasses and pouring a few ounces of different beers from the same style for a head-to-head comparison. It's really the best way to learn the flavor nuances and pick your favorites from the crowd.

The expansive space includes a large outdoor patio, a mezzanine level that overlooks the action, and a kitchen that makes small plates, sandwiches, and entrees. The fresh-baked pretzels and fries with house seasoning are popular, just like the southern chicken sandwich and Colorado beef burger.

FRESHCRAFT

1530 Blake St., Denver, CO 80202; (303) 758-9608; Freshcraft.com
Taps: 20+ **Bottles/cans:** 100+

Freshcraft fills a niche as a nicer beer bar with good food. And its prime downtown location, close to all the action, makes it one of the most visited beer bars in Denver. Freshcraft was founded by three brothers, Lucas, Aaron, and Jason Forgy, in 2010. The bar prides itself on a changing selection of more than two dozen craft beer taps and a bottle list that numbers close to 100.

The bar sits at the front and easily gets crowded. TV screens above the taps show the rotating beer list. A row of intimate booths line the wall, and a large room in the back can accept big parties who want to watch the game. In the warm months, the small sidewalk patio is a great place to take in downtown Denver.

Food is an important part of the Freshcraft business. The seasonal menu is of a higher quality than you'll find at other bars in the city, and it is designed largely to pair well with beer; the menu offers style recommendations under each item. The southern fried pickles on the appetizer menu are a go-to, just like the beer-crusted cheese dippers. Main plates range from cheese-crusted, Iowa-style pork tenderloin to stout spaghetti puttanesca. The lunch specials will entice beer drinking at the noon hour, so beware.

GOED ZUUR

2801 Welton St., Denver CO 80205; (720) 749-2709; GoedZuur.com
Taps: 26 **Bottles/cans:** 100+

Goed Zuur stands as a testament to Denver's elevated beer scene. The beautiful Five Points bar, located in a restored 1920s building near a light-rail stop, claims the mantle of the world's first sour beer taproom. The menu offers almost exclusively wild and sour beers. The fact that such a place can exist in Denver speaks to the city's educated consumers who were bred on craft beer.

The bar's name means "good acid" in Dutch, and the owners play on the Americanized pronunciation, which sounds like "goad zer." The elevated menu, paired with lofty prices to match, features the best sour beer makers from Colorado and the world with more than two dozen drafts and a bottle list unlike any other. The copper-topped bar, exposed rafters, and brick walls all lend elegance to the place, and a row of decanters—yes, it's that fancy—sit above a custom draft tower. A few nonsour beers are usually available, too.

The specialty beers from around the world are paired with custom plates of charcuterie, cheeses, and fresh-baked bread as well as entrees. The foodies in the group will want to grab a seat at the chef's counter and pair a funky cheese to go with a sour beer. The beer-wise staff will even walk you through a guided tasting.

HOPS & PIE

3920 Tennyson St., Denver, CO 80212; (303) 477-7000; hopsandpie.com
Taps: 11 **Bottles/cans:** 50+

Located on the popular Tennyson Street in Denver's Berkeley neighborhood, Hops & Pie is one of the city's beer and food treasures. The restaurant and bar pours some 20 different craft beers from across the state and country, often luring hard-to-find kegs from breweries that you can't easily taste in Colorado. To help cover the most ground, order a round of small tasting pours. Or go the opposite direction with a big bomber or large-format bottle from the 10-page cellar list. The locals know to join the beer club and not to miss the minifestivals. The events occur every few months, and Hops & Pie will dedicate their taps to the best and rarest beers in a particular style, whether hops, sours, stouts, or even pumpkin beers.

What puts the small pizzeria in a different class compared to other beer bars is the food. The hand-tossed pizzas are among the best you'll find in Denver, and the artisan pie of the month is always a creative twist that never disappoints. It's hard to build your own pizza here because the toppings are so endless, featuring eight cheeses, 12 meats, and a list of vegetables that includes dollops of mashed potatoes. If pizza isn't what you want, Hops & Pie also makes one of the best mac and cheese dishes. It includes smoked ham, English peas, herbed bread crumbs, and naturally, IPA. Whatever you choose, save room for a "super treat" with peanut butter Captain Crunch, Coco Puffs, and marshmallows.

STAR BAR DENVER

2137 Larimer St., Denver, CO 80205; (720) 328-2420;
StarBarDenver.com
Taps: 18 Bottles/cans: 20+

If you need a dive bar or hanker for karaoke, then Star Bar is the fix. The low-ceiling, dim-lit neighborhood bar with a back patio oozes old-Denver charm. And it's located on a street that is home to well-worn watering holes. Star Bar actually is one of the oldest bars in the city, dating to 1959. It went through a renovation in 2010, but it's hard to notice.

The winner of numerous awards for its dive status, Star Bar pours 14 taps of mostly Colorado craft beer and often features one-off or unusual beers. But you won't find pretentious beer drinkers here. The bar still pours what it calls "Colorado Kool-Aid," otherwise known as Coors Banquet and Coors Light. Star Bar also specializes in local craft spirits, with more than 30 on the wall. The bartenders are ready to mix the two specialties and make an interesting craft beer cocktail if you want, too. The bar is the after-party for plenty of downtown events, including GABF. It opens two hours before every home baseball game and features four taps on the back patio. But it's best to visit when it's dark and Larimer Street is alive with throngs of young downtowners, the kind of night where you want a beer that tastes good.

TERMINAL BAR

1701 Wynkoop St., Denver, CO 80211; (720) 460-3701;
TerminalBarDenver.com
Taps: 30 Bottles/cans: 2

The coolest beer spot in Denver is not a bar at all: it's a train station. Terminal Bar is located in the majestic Union Station, a 120-year-old landmark that underwent a $54 million renovation and reopened in 2014. It still beckons you with a neon sign to "travel by train." The bar is located in the historic ticketing office in the Great Hall, surrounded by a hotel, coffee and ice cream shops, restaurants, and a cocktail lounge. The patio outside is a place to watch the downtown bustle, and inside the dimmed bar, there are booths and a lengthy counter with stools to order beer, wine, and cocktails. But skip both and order in the hall from the ticket window framed by menus with 30 Colorado craft brews that collectively represent a broad cross section of the state's beer scene. (The actual ticket window is down one of the side halls.) The brewery list usually includes Left Hand, Epic, Crooked Stave, and River North.

Drink a pint in the station to watch travelers walk through with ski bags and suitcases as they arrive by train from the airport and commuters catch a bus or light-rail car to the suburbs. The hall features communal tables, comfy couches, train benches, and two table shuffleboards. It comes alive from noon to midnight with a rotating cast of characters.

WALTER'S 303 PIZZERIA & PUBLIK HOUSE

1906 Pearl St., Denver, CO 80203; (303) 864-9000; Walters 303.com
Taps: 30 **Bottles/cans:** 12+

Walter's 303 Pizzeria & Publik House in downtown Denver is a secret gem in Denver's craft beer world. And one look online at the tap list will prompt you to head there immediately. The reason: Walter's 303 manages to get beers you can't find elsewhere in the city, which is impressive given the other great beer bars listed in this section. It's a small pizza joint with a long bar and a handful of high-top tables in the Uptown neighborhood of Denver. The company also operates locations in Littleton and Colorado Springs, but the best beer is found in Denver. The owners know the industry and hand-select each keg to keep the taps exceptional.

The 30 draft lines are constantly changing, and the beer board will helpfully tell you which is about to empty next so you can plot your journey. (If you can't decide, the bartenders will roll a dice with 30 numbers on it to pick for you.) The rare and barrel-aged offerings from Colorado and the nation's best breweries are great, but there's also plenty of other styles to satisfy that friend who just wants to drink a Boulevard Brewing Tank 7. The cheese bread is addictive, so be careful when ordering, and the pizzas hit the spot. So now you know the secret.

Denver Area
Arvada, Aurora, Broomfield, Castle Rock, Golden, Littleton, and Lone Tree

Much like the city, the sprawling suburbs and towns in the Denver metropolitan area are seeing their own craft beer boom. Here the trend favors neighborhood breweries, ones that serve the locals and don't worry much about distribution to a wider audience. It's a throwback to the old days when a family would run a metal pail to the brewery on the corner and fill it with local beer. Now, we call those growlers—and no spillage or kids are involved. The idea still holds, though. To taste these great breweries, you need to travel outside the city limits, whether to the foothills of Golden or the commercial centers of Aurora and Castle Rock.

The breweries in this section make it worth the trip. And don't let the neighborhood moniker make you think the beer is less tasty. Most bedroom communities outside Denver host numerous quality craft brewers and beer bars, and a new class of up-and-comers is just behind them. A handful of the breweries are perfect stops on the way to Red Rocks Amphitheatre or on the way back from the mountain biking and hiking trails. And there's Coors Brewing Company in Golden,

ONCE A CULT BREWERY ITSELF BUT NOW A MEGABREWING POWERHOUSE. BRECKENRIDGE BREWERY, WHICH IS PART OF THE BUDWEISER FAMILY, ALSO IS LOCATED OUTSIDE DENVER NOW. IT BUILT A DESTINATION BREWERY IN LITTLETON. BOTH BREWERS MAY DRAW THE SNEERS FROM CRAFT BEER PURISTS, BUT FOR MOST IN COLORADO, THEY REMAIN A POINT OF PRIDE AND A SOURCE FOR WELL-MADE BEER.

BRECKENRIDGE BREWERY

2920 Brewery Ln., Littleton, CO 80120; (844) 682-7325; BreckBrew.com
600 S. Main St., Breckenridge, CO 80424; (904) 453-1550
Founded: 1990 **Founder:** Richard Squire **Brewer:** Todd Usry
Flagship beers: Avalanche Amber, Hop Peak IPA, Vanilla Porter, Agave Wheat, Mango Mosaic Pale Ale, Oatmeal Stout, Breck Lager **Seasonals/special releases:** Nitro Vanilla Porter, Nitro Orange Cream Ale, Summer Pils, Autumn Ale, Christmas Ale, Snow Glare Hoppy Wheat Ale, 471 Small Batch Double IPA, 72 Imperial Chocolate Cream Stout, Brewery Lane Barrel Aged series, 471 IPA Barrel series, Stranahan's Well-Built **Tours:** Thurs through Mon, 11 a.m., 1, 3, and 5 p.m. Reservations required **Taproom hours:** Sun through Thurs, 11 a.m. to 10 p.m.; Fri, 11 a.m. to 11 p.m.; Sat, 10 a.m. to 11 p.m. Growlers and bottled beers to go.

In 1990, practiced homebrewer Richard Squire opened the third craft brewery in Colorado in the popular ski town of Breckenridge. The aptly named Breckenridge Brewery was a small affair, built with locals and visiting skiers in mind. It was an overnight success, and in 1992, the brewery opened a second brewpub in Denver in a run-down area that transformed a few years later with the opening of the nearby Coors Field baseball stadium. The brewery soon outgrew that space and moved production to a larger facility at 471 Kalamath St., south of downtown.

In 2015, the big move came. Breckenridge built a destination brewery, a farmhouse-inspired estate, and moved to its current home in Littleton. The 12-acre property is the site of an old farm but now hosts a massive 100-barrel brew house, a restaurant, and a beer garden. The ski town brewpub remains, too. But the entire Breckenridge brand is now owned by international conglomerate Anheuser-Busch InBev.

The earth-shattering sale in 2016, to a big beer company that insults craft brewing, tarnished Breckenridge in the minds of some beer fans, but the place remains a hallmark of the state's beer community. The **Avalanche Amber Ale** is an ode to craft brewing's early days, and the **471 Small Batch**, a double IPA, remains a legacy of its time in Denver. To keep relevant, the brewery is making barrel-aged and limited beers for its **Brewery Lane series**, which includes an imperial version of its famous vanilla porter aged in rum barrels. Another recent series took the 471 IPA and aged it in barrels with different dry-hop variations.

The new location also hosts a huge summer concert series and special beer dinners.

CANNONBALL CREEK BREWING COMPANY

393 N. Washington Ave., Golden, CO 80403; (303) 278-0111; CannonballCreekBrewing.com
Founded: 2013 **Founders:** Jason Stengl and Brian Hutchinson
Brewer: Jonathan Lee **Flagship beers:** Featherweight Pale Ale, Mindbender IPA, Trump Hands IPA, Solid Gold Belgian Golden, Brickyard Porter **Seasonals/special releases:** Let's Talk about Mex, Rosemary Sourdough Saison, Vienna Lager, Felix Da Stout **Tour:** None **Taproom hours:** Mon through Wed, 3 to 10 p.m.; Thurs, 3 to 11 p.m.; Fri and Sat, noon to 11 p.m.; Sun, noon to 10 p.m.

Cannonball Creek Brewing is golden, all the way through. The founders, Jason Stengl and Brian Hutchinson, left Mountain Sun breweries in Boulder and opened their own operation in their hometown of Golden in 2013. The brewery took the original name for Clear Creek, which runs through the former gold rush town. In its first five years, the brewery took home eight GABF medals, including two golds.

The early recognition—particularly for its hoppy beers—makes the small Cannonball Creek a must-visit destination. Located west of Denver, it sits along a highway that runs the length of the foothills north toward Boulder, making it an easy stop for outdoor adventurers coming down from the mountains. Most the

cars in the parking lot are toting bikes or roof racks loaded with gear, and hiking boots inside the taproom are the norm. The brewery is located in a commercial strip, but it makes the best with the space with an open taproom often filled with neighbors and families playing board games, a food truck pulled up most every day, and a patio that allows dogs to slumber under the umbrellas.

The first beer to order is the **Featherweight Pale Ale**, a multiple-award winner that achieves impressive balance with a bready Munich malt that counters the hop character and fruity aromatics. The new star of the show is **Trump Hands**, a session IPA with a tongue-in-cheek name referencing the size of the reality-TV-star-turned-president's digits. It won gold at GABF and the World Beer Cup—an incredibly impressive feat. The tap list rotates with the seasons, meaning there's a beer for each day you spend in the mountains, whether a Mexican lager in the hot summer or a Munich Dunkel for those fall days when the aspen trees turn gold.

COORS BREWING COMPANY/AC GOLDEN (MILLERCOORS)

1221 Ford St., Golden, CO 80401; (303) 277-2337; MillerCoors.com
Founded: 1873 **Founders:** Adolph Coors and Jacob Schueler
Brewers: Various **Flagship beers:** Coors Banquet, Coors Light and Blue Moon; Colorado Native Amber Lager, Golden Lager, IPL and Pilsner
Seasonals/special releases: Colorado Native Imperial Porter, Saison, Olathe, Winterfest, Kriek Noir, Peche, Plum **Tours and taproom hours:** Thurs through Mon, 10 a.m. to 4 p.m.

The best place to start at Coors is the 40-minute, self-guided, free tour that hundreds of thousands of people enjoy each year when they visit the brewery in Golden. Founded in 1893, Coors is one the oldest and most storied breweries in America and a pillar of the nation's beer history. Located in an old frontier town, it stands as the world's largest brewery in a single location. The size of the facility is humbling by any standard, and it's worth the eye-opening tour, where the vast economies of scale come into view.

The precision process is undeniably breathtaking, even for those that abhor fizzy yellow beer. Coors malts most of its own grains, a feat few breweries around the world can claim. It processes its own water, sourced from nearby mountain springs. It grows much of its own hops. And it produces its own cans. Coors was the first brewery to use aluminum cans for beer in America. One of

the most impressive sights is the farm of traditionally fashioned copper brew kettles that stretch as far as the eye can see.

Coors is not quite a local Colorado brand anymore given its international stature and reach, but Coors Banquet and Coors Light remain popular with native Coloradans. The MillerCoors family owns all sorts of brands now, including former craft brewers from across the country, and most are available in the tasting room after the tour. One brand to try is Colorado Native made by AC Golden, a stand-alone subsidiary that launched in 2007. The brewery uses

Beer Lover's Pick

COORS BANQUET

Style: American-Style Lager
ABV: 5 percent
Availability: Year-round on tap, in bottles, and in cans
Enjoying a fresh Coors Banquet brewed in Golden is an absolute must for any self-respecting beer fan visiting Colorado. Ask any brewer what beer they enjoy most, and you'll hear Banquet pretty often. It's one of the worst-kept secrets in the craft beer world. Few beers in America are as iconic or have been brewed in much the same way for so long. The bright, golden-blonde pale lager hits only 5 percent ABV and remains as quaffable and clean as you expect.

three 30-barrel copper kettles imported from Germany that are located in the middle of the larger brewery. Most of the beers use 100 percent Colorado-grown hops. It's not all lagers, either. The barrel-aged sour beers are not to be missed.

DRY DOCK BREWING COMPANY

South Dock: 15120 E. Hampden Ave., Aurora, CO 80014; (303) 400-5606; DryDockBrewing.com; Taproom hours: Mon through Thurs, noon to 10 p.m.; Fri, noon to 11 p.m.; Sat, 11 a.m. to 11 p.m.; Sun, 11 a.m. to 10 p.m.
North Dock: 2801 Tower Rd., Aurora, CO 80011; Taproom hours: Wed and Thurs, 2 to 8 p.m.; Fri and Sat, noon to 8 p.m.
Founded: 2005 **Founders:** Kevin DeLange and Michele Reding
Brewer: Alan Simons **Flagship beers:** Apricot Blonde, Sour Apricot, IPA, Hop Abomination, Grapefruit Double IPA, Amber Ale, Vanilla Porter
Seasonals/special releases: Wheat Beer, Docktoberfest, Coffee Stout, Double Apricot Blonde, Bligh's Barleywine Ale, Coconut Belgian Dark, Pumpkin Double Porter, Imperial Stout **Tours:** Sat, 2 p.m., at the North Dock location **Taprooms:** Growlers at South Dock, crowlers at North Dock, and cans and bottles at both locations to go

D ry Dock Brewing Company in Aurora is the brainchild of homebrew store owner Kevin DeLange. In 2005, he expanded the shop to add a seven-barrel brew system. Like many brewers, he quickly discovered that success in

brewing means you rapidly run out of room. In 2009, he moved into a bigger space and the same year Dry Dock won the Small Brewery of the Year award at GABF. Dry Dock opened a second location as a dedicated production brewery in 2013. Now both boast taprooms. The original location in an Aurora strip mall is known as South Dock and still includes the attached homebrew store, where you can shop while sipping a pint for inspiration. The production facility, which offers tours and its own tasting room, is known as North Dock.

Brewed-to-style perfection is the best way to describe the majority of Dry Dock's beers. But that's not to say there aren't plenty of creative flourishes. **Apricot Blonde** is one of the best-known beers in the state and a year-round burst of sunshine with fruit flavor but a crisp finish. The **Vanilla Porter**, loaded with vanilla beans, is another staple. The beer loudly and proudly announces its vanilla addition with sweet aroma and flavors of toffee, malted milk balls, molasses, and wafer cookies.

Beer Lover's Pick

BLIGH'S BARLEYWINE ALE

Style: English Barleywine
ABV: 10.5 percent
Availability: Limited fourth-quarter release in 22-ounce bottles

Debuting in 2011, Bligh's Barleywine Ale was featured on many "best beers" lists in Colorado from the start and remains a favorite. Bligh's is a hazelnut brown–colored English-style barley-wine aged for seven months in whiskey barrels. The beer breathes welcoming aromas of leather, vanilla, fig, currants, black tea, molasses, and sherry. On the palate, the flavor of black licorice is present with secondary notes of plum, muscovado sugar, black treacle, and baked apples. In keeping with tradi-tional English barleywine style, the beer is very sweet with low bitterness and a hint of alcohol.

Dry Dock Brewing Company

FOUR NOSES BREWING COMPANY

8855 W. 116th Circle, #4, Broomfield, CO 80021; (720) 460-2797; 4NosesBrewing.com
Founded: 2014 **Founders:** Tommy, David, Jessica, and Natan Bibliowicz **Brewers:** Tommy Bibliowicz, Alex Rabe, and Andrew Faron **Flagship beers:** 'Bout Damn Time, Raspberry Blonde Ale, Whimsy New England IPA series, Velvet Milkshake IPA series, Perfect Drift Pilsner **Seasonals/special releases:** Bubblin, Ad Hoc series, Oktoberfest, Pump Action Pumpkin Ale, Ryeciprocal **Tours:** On request **Taproom hours:** Mon through Thurs, 3 to 10 p.m.; Fri, noon to 11 p.m.; Sat, 10 a.m. to 11 p.m.; Sun, 11 a.m. to 10 p.m. Growlers, crowlers, bottles, and cans to go.

N oses" in the name refers to the four family members who envisioned the brewery at a pub in Ireland over pints of Guinness. (There was also four dogs between them.) For the family, beer is a uniting favorite. Natan Bibliowicz, the patriarch, taught his son Tommy to brew, and what started as a bonding exercise became a shared family passion. Tommy Bibliowicz leads the operation, and his brother David, an architect like their father, hand sketches the designs for the beer labels.

Four Noses is located in a nondescript warehouse-sized building in Broomfield, a suburb between Denver and Boulder that makes it an easy pit stop for beer fans.

Four Noses made a mark with its **'Bout Damn Time**, an American IPA with Pacific Northwest hops that is too easy to drink at 7.1 percent. And exemplifying

Beer Lover's Pick

'BOUT DAMN TIME

Style: American IPA

ABV: 7.1 percent

Availability: Year-round on tap and in cans

Defying all expectations, Four Noses didn't make an American IPA for two years. So 'Bout Damn Time is appropriately named. Ironically, now most of the beer board is often dominated with hoppy beers. The first batch of 'Bout Damn Time sold out quickly, but the

Four Noses Brewing Company

brewers took about 10 iterations until the recipe hit just right. It's a West Coast style with mosaic and amarillo hops that is crisp and bitter but not overwhelming thanks to a simple but present malt character.

its ability to remain on trend, it branched into different series that showcase New England–style IPAs (**Whimsy**) and milkshake IPAs (**Velvet**). The newest direction for the brewery is the expansion of its mixed culture and wild sour beers. And whether you love or hate pumpkin beers—because it's often one or the other—Four Noses makes one of the best, the award-winning **Pump Action**, which comes around each fall.

HOLIDAILY BREWING COMPANY

801 Brickyard Circle, Golden, CO 80403; (303) 278-2337; HolidailyBrewing.com
Founded: 2016 **Founder:** Karen Hertz **Brewers:** Jacob Johnson and William Martinez **Flagship beers:** Fat Randy's IPA, Favorite Blonde and Stout **Seasonals/special releases:** Belgian Buckwit and Patchy Waters **Tours:** On request **Taproom hours:** Mon through Thurs, 2 to 9 p.m.; Fri, noon to 10 p.m.; Sat, 11 a.m. to 10 p.m.; Sun, 11 a.m. to 9 p.m. Growlers and cans to go.

The perception about gluten-free beer is that it's a less flavorful version of the real thing. But Holidaily Brewing in Golden is working to correct that idea. It is the only dedicated gluten-free brewery in Colorado and the concept of Karen Hertz, a craft beer enthusiast who worked in distribution at MillerCoors and became gluten free as part of her recovery after battling cancer. She thought that good gluten-free beers were hard to find, so she decided to open her own brewery.

For the gluten intolerant, barley, wheat and rye are nonstarters. And for the most sensitive, even the enzymes that many brewers use to remove or reduce gluten to imperceptible levels won't suffice. Holidaily doesn't use any of those ingredients at its brew house, instead making most of its beers with millet and buckwheat. Even though the operation looks pretty standard, the brewery boasts that its initial 10-barrel system is unlike anything in the world and specifically designed for these types of beers.

The niche allowed the brewery to grow fast—moving from three beers on tap to 10 in two years and then expanding with distribution of the light **Favorite Blonde**, **Fat Randy's IPA**, and a stout in 16-ounce cans. Sours and even barrel-aged beers are the newest direction for Holidaily.

LONE TREE BREWING COMPANY

8200 Park Meadows Dr., #8222, Lone Tree, CO 80124; (303) 792-5822; LoneTreeBrewingCo.com
Founded: 2011 **Founders:** John Winter and Jason Wiedmaier
Brewer: Josh West **Flagship beers:** Mexican Lager, Red Ale, Double IPA, Peach Pale Ale, Pale Ale **Seasonals/special releases:** Cucumber Wheat, Vanilla Caramel Amber, Triple IPA, Biere de Printemps, India Pale Lager, Cranberry Saison, English Old Ale, Horchata Stout, Hop Zombie **Tours:** On request **Taproom hours:** Mon, noon to 8 p.m.; Tues and Wed, noon to 9 p.m.; Thurs and Fri, noon to 10 p.m.; Sat, 11 a.m. to 10 p.m.; Sun, 11 a.m. to 8 p.m. Growlers, bottles, and cans to go.

Lone Tree Brewing Company opened for business in December 2011 as a craft beer haven near a shopping mall in the suburb of Lone Tree, about 20 minutes south of Denver. The brewery is located in a bright and spacious retail and business park, but it retains a family-friendly neighborhood feel with a steady flow of dedicated locals. Lone Tree's founding partners, John Winter and Jason Wiedmaier, started small but now distribute across the state and into neighboring Kansas.

The brewery pours five year-round beers and releases new ales or lagers each month, often keeping with the seasons. Most of the beers for distribution fit traditional styles, leaning on a European influence, but the taproom offers a handful of experimental or innovative brews to keep things interesting. Most of the beers are lower in alcohol content, making them approachable and

Beer Lover's Pick

VANILLA CARAMEL AMBER

Style: Amber Ale
ABV: 6 percent
Availability: Fall seasonal on tap and in cans

For weeks before its release, the calls demanding Vanilla Caramel Amber begin to inundate the Lone Tree taproom. It arrives in October, a signal that the leaves are changing and the winter flakes are not far behind. The amber beer stands out for its heavy use of caramel malts to lend the flavor in the name without adding extra sugars or candies. And it's one of the only in its category that uses vanilla beans without making it too sweet.

easy-drinking. One exception is a limited-release beer that appears every fall, the award-winning **Hop Zombie Imperial Red IPA**. The beer can draw lines, and the bottles don't last long. The old-school style is reinvented with New Zealand motueka hops, which give it an earthy and piney bite. The **English Old Ale** showcases the brewery's work best with a traditional British style available each October that warms the soul with gingerbread flavors of cinnamon, allspice, and nutmeg.

NEW IMAGE BREWING

5622 Yukon St., Arvada, CO 80002; (720) 900-5620; NIBrewing.com; Taproom hours: Mon through Wed, 3 to 10 p.m.; Thurs, 11 a.m. to 10 p.m.; Fri, 11 a.m. to midnight; Sat 11 a.m. to midnight; Sun, noon to 10 p.m.
9505 W. 44th Ave., Wheat Ridge, CO 80033
Founded: 2015 **Founders:** Brandon Capps and Sean Fisher **Brewers:** Brandon Capps and Kyle Rindahl **Flagship beers:** Flora, Dyad, East Coast Transplant, Single By Choice, The Coriolis Effect **Seasonals/special releases:** Paul, Melanoidin, Wood, One More Time, Pay It Forward **Tours:** None. Crowlers and cans to go.

New Image Brewing's Brandon Capps made his mark in Colorado with his **East Coast Transplant**, a hazy IPA that spoke to his roots as a brewer in Pittsburgh. Next came the kombucha-style sour **Dyad** with a mixed-culture fermentation that showcases elements of both beverages. Then he started a spontaneously fermented beer program alongside more barrel aging. And he's developing oak-fermented lagers at the same time as dessert beers. The goal of all the experimentation is to keep pushing the limits. One day, Capps, an engineer who started in the industry at Anheuser-Busch, wants New Image to be the one creating the trends.

The beer menu inside the downtown Arvada location shows the brewery's creativity. It's located near a light-rail stop on a line that connects to Denver. And a few miles south in neighboring Wheat Ridge, New Image is expanding into a much larger production facility that can crank out more beers in a wider footprint. The brewery cans a wide variety of its beers and distributes to select beer stores in the area. Both locations also serve food, with the Arvada brewpub focusing on elevated tacos and world cuisine.

Even with the increasing popularity and growth, the brewery remains connected to the community. It partners with a local nonprofit focused on

Beer Lover's Pick

DYAD

Style: Brett Saison
ABV: 7.5 percent
Availability: Year-round on tap and in cans
Dyad is a great example of how New Image thinks outside the box. The beer started as a blend of kombucha and Brett saison—two tart, quenching liquids that blend to create a better combination. Now, the recipe is more integrated with the bacteria and yeast that ferments kombucha, and the tea that gives it flavor, added to the beer to create something more elegant. The variants include eye-opening flavors like blackberry and cream, strawberry lemonade, and coconut lime.

New Image Brewing Company

mental health issues, donating proceeds from one of its beers to a cause that is personal for Capps, who is keen on social impact businesses.

NEW TERRAIN BREWING COMPANY

16401 Table Mountain Pkwy., Golden, CO 80403; (720) 697-7848; NewTerrainBrewing.com
Founded: 2016 **Founders:** Josh and Kaylee Robbins **Brewers:** Josh Robbins and John Law **Flagship beers:** Lost, Golden Haze, Hoppatropica, Suntrip, Rambler **Seasonals/special releases:** Shadowland, Mirage, North Star series, Key Largo, Rubus Deliciosus **Tours:** Sat and Sun, noon **Taproom hours:** Mon through Wed, noon to 9 p.m.; Thurs and Fri, noon to 10 p.m.; Sat 11 a.m. to 10 p.m.; Sun, 11 a.m. to 9 p.m. Growlers, crowlers, and cans to go.

The most popular way to get to New Terrain Brewing is on bike. Located at the foot of the popular Table Mountain, near the trail up the flank and not far from the Golden Bike Park, it's a perfect place to end a ride. The gorgeous brew house, a mix of reclaimed wood and red sandstone brick that blends with the surroundings, even shares a building with a local bicycle manufacturer.

Brewer and founder Josh Robbins applies the idea of wandering in the outdoors to making beer by not being bound to tradition too much. The beer menu evolves and often features different iterations as the brewers play with a recipe. There are plenty of light beers—like the refreshing **Rubus Deliciosus**, a

raspberry wit, and the **Key Largo**, a key lime kölsch—if you stop in the warmer months. Or grab a rich **Shadowland** stout when its colder.

For those who like hops, New Terrain is the place to find a "Colorado IPA." More than a moniker, it's listed as a style on the brewery's board. The name of the beer, called **Lost**, speaks to its wandering sensibilities between two places—East and West Coast IPAs. Robbins describes it as "fruity and dank," a hybrid of the two noted styles. The beer is golden in color without being super hazy. It starts with fruit notes in the aroma and finishes with the resiny bitterness that is firm but not too much. Order a Colorado IPA and the New England–style **Golden Haze**. Then start a debate about whether Colorado IPA deserves its own style or merely is a product of state pride.

ROCKYARD AMERICAN GRILL & BREWING COMPANY

880 Castleton Rd., Castle Rock, CO 80109; (303) 814-9273; Rockyard.com
Founded: 1999 **Founders:** Jeff Drabing and Mike Drabing **Brewers:** Zac Rissmiller, Derick Rivera, and John Schneider **Flagship beers:** Spring Loaded, Rugged Grind, Orange Moon Rising, Hopalypto, Primadonna, Plum Creek Buoyant **Seasonals/special releases:** Slightly Sessionable, Bourbon Barrel Stout **Tours:** None **Taproom hours:** Mon through Sun, 11 a.m. to 10 p.m. Growlers and cans to go.

As expected from a brewpub owned by siblings, there is a distinct family-oriented vibe at Rockyard Brewing Company. Opened in 1999, it's a stalwart in Castle Rock, about 30 miles south of Denver, and retains a classic tavern feel with a long, dark bar and plenty of TVs. It's the longest-running brewpub in a place with minimal beer options, and it offers a hideout from the sprawling outlet mall and shopping district just across the way. A perk: The brewery cans and distributes, meaning you can even take what you like to go.

The beers are generally lower in alcohol, possibly a reflection that you need to drive to get to it. And most are traditional with an emphasis on German styles rather than experimental, with wits, blondes, ambers, and more. A handful of the beers are executed to the book and win awards to prove it. The hop-forward German pilsner dubbed **Primadonna** took gold at the World Beer Cup. Another recent award winner is a barrel-aged sour called **Plum Creek**. The **Buoyant** is fast becoming a popular beer, a boysenberry blonde ale that isn't overly fruited and is served on the spritzy side like fruited seltzer water.

The food at Rockyard is the standard variety and covers a lot of ground with nachos and wings, burgers and sandwiches, pasta and seafood, steak and enchiladas, and pizzas and calzones. A special is the cream of jalapeño soup.

YAK & YETI RESTAURANT & BREWPUB (SPICE TRADE BREWING)

7803 Ralston Rd., Arvada, CO 80002; (303) 431-9000; TheYakandYeti.com
Founded: 2008 Founders: Dol Bhattarrai and Jeff Tyler Brewer: Jeff Tyler Flagship beers: Chai Milk Stout, Sun Temple IPA Seasonals/special releases: Changes Tours: None Restaurant hours: Mon through Sat, 11 a.m. to 9:30 p.m.; Sun, 11 a.m. to 9 p.m.

Yak & Yeti is an oddity—a Indian and Nepalese brewpub. The unlikely combination actually makes a lot of sense. Indian food, in its many and varied spicy formats, is a fine and complementary companion to styles of malty and hoppy ales and lagers. Located in the suburb of Arvada, the brewpub is situated in a 150-year-old house with dining rooms on the first and second floors. Great Indian food isn't always easy to find, but the curries, various rice-based dishes, and naan breads meet high standards and pair nicely with the 12 tap lines.

The restaurant operated a brewpub under its name for years but decided in 2017 to separate the beer operation and recast it as Spice Trade Brewing. The new name, in part, relates to a trademark dispute with Great Divide Brewing concerning the word "Yeti." But the new brand also gives the beer its own platform, and the owners boosted production and are now distributing. The brews still draw inspiration from the culinary side. The house **Chai Milk Stout** is a good example. Made with a house blend of spices, the aroma is huge. In the taste, all the spices are present but do not overwhelm the core roasty and chocolate stout characteristics. The brewery always is trying new things, whether it's a peanut butter and banana nut brown or a New England IPA, the latter being a nod to the brewer's favorite style. Yak & Yeti also operates three additional restaurants—in Denver, Brighton, and Westminster—that offer Spice Trade beers but do not brew on-site.

COLORADO PLUS BREW PUB, TAP HOUSE AND RESTAURANT

6995 W. 38th Ave., Wheat Ridge, CO 80033; (720) 353-4853; ColoradoPlus.net
Taps: 56

Colorado Plus is a jack of all trades. It's a beer bar with 56 rotating taps. It's a brewpub that offers nearly 10 of its own beers. And it's a restaurant with a focus on local ingredients. All these characteristics make it hard to categorize but great to visit.

The seemingly infinite row of shining silver tap handles behind the bar is what makes the Wheat Ridge establishment notable. The beer menu is an impressive ode to Colorado given that all the taps are home-state brews and cover the full range of styles year-round. The beer buyers have established relationships with local breweries, an advantage that gives them the ability to score the hard-to-find, one-off, interesting beers that so many other bars never get to pour.

Given the dedication to Colorado, it's probably not a surprise that the brewer, James Coulter, spent his whole life in the state, making the transition

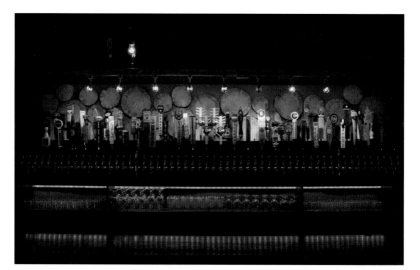

from a videographer and producer to homebrewing. His brews ran the gamut on a recent visit, from a bold barleywine to a Nordic ale brewed with local honey and rose hips. The food is a local creation, too. Most of the ingredients are sourced from local and regional farms, and the kitchen makes a menu from scratch that ranges from a white cheddar and pork belly macaroni to fresh-never-frozen chicken wings and bison burgers. Altogether, it makes Colorado Plus a rare find not too far west of Denver.

JAKE'S BREW BAR AND BEER GARDEN

2530 W. Main St., Littleton, CO 80120; (303) 996-1006;
JakesBrewBar.com
Taps: 36 Bottles/cans: 30+

The sprawling community of Littleton, nine miles south of Denver, is full of tightly packed neighborhoods, commercial centers, and wide roads. But take a minute, exit US 85, and head into Old Town to find a craft beer gem on Main Street tucked between professional offices and boutique stores.

Jake's is the bigger brother of a smaller operation that once was located next door as a beer bar–coffee shop combination. The decor is eclectic, if not just random, like a familiar neighborhood watering hole decorated by the regulars. Each of the upcycled tap handles is unique, and you can spend plenty of time sipping from your glass and deciphering the stories behind them. The beer list allows for a lengthy stay because you're sure to find a beer you haven't tried or the new go-to pint from a combination of local and US breweries.

On the pleasant days, grab a seat on the sidewalk patio or, better yet, head out back to the beer garden, where you'll find a fire pit, tables, and live music each Saturday night. The grill out back makes food on the weekends, and there are plans to add a food truck, too.

KLINE'S BEER HALL

7519 Grandview Ave., Arvada, CO 80002; (303) 351-7938;
KlinesBeerHall.com
Taps: 56

The sign on the inside wall says it all: "High Quality Beer Served Here." If you don't believe it, go check out the list of 56 tap beers. Kline's Beer Hall is just one more reason that downtown Arvada—with New Image Brewing and the Denver Beer Company, as well as other great bars and restaurants—is becoming a hip place to live.

The space is well lit from all the windows at the front and keeps an Olde Towne Arvada feel with the brick walls and exposed rafters. The place is named, sort of, after Andrian Klein, who received the first beer license in Arvada in 1993. The tap menu features great out-of-state breweries as well as the best from within Colorado. If you join their e-mail list for the Secret Keg Club, you'll even get notified when a special tap gets poured just for the members. The tap wall is long and includes a dozen light beers, a handful of malt wonders, a plurality of hoppy beers, and even a good numbers of sours.

The food menu is focused on sausages to pair with beers, but it extends to appetizers like bacon jam and pierogi as well as rotisserie chicken and baked mac and cheese.

PARRY'S PIZZERIA & CRAFT BEER BAR

Various locations in the Denver area; ParrysPizza.com
Taps: 40 to 100

A pizza chain, even if it's a local outfit, is not quite the place you'd expect to find great craft beer. Most of the time, pizza pairs with pitchers, and generally the beer skews toward the lighter and less flavorful end of the spectrum. This is why Parry's Pizzeria is so different. The chain has eight locations in Colorado, six of them concentrated in the Denver area, including Northglenn, Centennial, and Highlands Ranch.

The initial Parker, Castle Rock, and Greenwood Village locations have great taps but fewer of them. Each of the newer locations trumpet at least 100 beers on draft. And it's not just any beer but a well-curated list of great breweries and styles that recently included a sour from Russian River Brewing and double IPA from Port Brewing alongside the best of local brews. There are staples, too, such as **Avery White Rascal**. The company dedicates a beer buyer to keeping the list fresh and different at each location. Look for plenty of beer-tasting events, too. Epic Brewing makes a handful of beers exclusively for Parry's. And the $4 pints that rotate each month are a huge draw.

The pizza is New York–style. The cheese pizza fits the bill with "the true taste and smell of NY pie," as the menu suggests. Other items include salads, calzones, and sandwiches, but Parry's says the fan favorites are the hot wings and fried dough parm bites.

Boulder

Home to the University of Colorado's flagship campus, Boulder fits the bill as a typical liberal college town. It's nestled at the foot of the mountains near the iconic Flatirons, the jagged flanks of sedimentary rock that titled open like a drawbridge to make room for the Rocky Mountains millions of years ago. The downtown pedestrian mall along Pearl Street is filled with outdoor shops, street performers, and beer spots. More recently, the city's image is maturing as it becomes a hub for tech companies and the affluent who, like everyone else, are drawn to the outdoors. The brewing scene reflects the city's vibe, offering upscale confines and beautiful, shiny breweries to beer spots that qualify as start-ups. Boulder is a place that likes beer. It's home to the first craft brewery in Colorado, Boulder Beer Company. When it started back 1979, there were only 42 other breweries operating in the nation. The most recognized beer name in Boulder is now Avery Brewing, one of the big players in the brewing world and proud owner of a massive brew house to the north of the city. With all this beer, perhaps it's not a surprise that the Brewers Association, the craft beer industry's trade association, also calls Boulder home.

AVERY BREWING COMPANY

**4910 Nautilus Ct. N, Boulder CO 80301; (303) 440-4324;
AveryBrewing.com**
Founded: 1993 **Founder:** Adam Avery **Brewer:** Fred Rizzo **Flagship
beers:** Avery IPA, White Rascal, El Gose, Liliko'i Kepolo, Go Play IPA,
Real Peel IPA, Maharaja IPA, Ellie's Brown, Hog Heaven, The Reverend
Seasonals/special releases: Raspberry Sour, Vanilla Bean Stout,
Tangerine Quad, Apricot Sour, Coconut Porter, Ginger Sour, Bug Zapper,
The Kaiser, Old Jubilation Ale, Plank'D, Tweak, Uncle Jacob's Stout,
Rumpkin **Tours:** Mon through Fri, 4 p.m.; Sat, 2 and 3:30 p.m.; Sun,
2 p.m. **Taproom hours:** Mon, 3 to 10 p.m.; Tues through Sun, 11:30
a.m. to 11 p.m. Growlers, bottles, and cans to go.

Adam Avery founded his namesake brewery in 1993 with a seven-barrel
brew house tucked away in a small industrial corner of Boulder. Now, the
brewery sprawls 67,000 square feet on a 5.6-acre parcel with four behemoth
720-barrel fermentation tanks. How times change. The new digs, built in 2015
for more than $30 million, are a far cry from when Avery won its first GABF
medal for Out of Bounds Stout a year after it opened and when it first packaged

an IPA in the state in 1996. The story of Avery's rise to craft beer stardom epitomizes the industry's trajectory. In November 2017, Adam and his father, Larry Avery, sold a 30 percent stake in the company to Mahou San Miguel, a family-owned Spanish megabrewer, to help enable more growth.

Under the Brewers Association's industry guidelines, Avery no longer qualifies as independent craft beer. But unlike some craft brewers who partnered with big beer, the deal did little to lessen the brewery's stock in the market. Avery remains an icon in the Colorado beer world with a packed taproom and sold-out festivals. The larger brewery did not change Avery's approach to beer—it's still as extreme and eccentric as ever, from the boozy barrel-aged stouts to the complex sours. Some of the unusual beers make it to mass distribution, but the brewery is where you can try even more with the taproom-only series. Order from the great restaurant menu and try as many as you can.

The bar downstairs features 30 taps, and another 30 are located upstairs in a dining room next to the gift shop. The locals know to check on weekends to see if a third bar, hidden at the end of the catwalk that overlooks the brewing operation, is open for even more exclusive beers. Regardless

Beer Lover's Pick

OLD JUBILATION ALE

Style: Old Ale
ABV: 8.3 percent
Availability: Sept through Dec on tap and in bottles

The big barrel–aged stouts at Avery are amazing. The fruity and bitter IPAs the brewery makes are essentials. But there's something about Old Jubilation that just hits the spot. In a can and still cellarable, this English strong ale is as good a signal of the winter season as snow. It hits 8.3 percent ABV and pours the color of mahogany with a beautiful caramel aroma and a body that  evokes the flavors of a well-stocked spice rack despite containing no spices at all. This is a beer designed to let the malts do most of the talking.

Avery Brewing Company

of where it pours, the **White Rascal** is a Colorado staple, an easy-drinking Belgian white ale that pairs with food or a hike. The second must-taste, from-the-source beer is **Maharaja**, an old-school imperial IPA that is a bitter bomb with a malt base and alcohol tinge at 9 percent to match. If you're still standing, the barrel-series stouts, like **Tweak** and **Dui Cochi**, should be next. And look in the gift shop cooler for special bottles from the series that you can buy only at the brewery.

BOULDER BEER COMPANY

Wilderness Pub; 2880 Wilderness Place, Boulder, CO 80301; (303) 444-8448; BoulderBeer.com; Taproom hours: Mon through Sun, 11 a.m. to 10 p.m.
Boulder Beer on Walnut; 1123 Walnut St., Boulder, CO 80302; Taproom hours: Mon through Sun, 11 to 2 a.m.
Founded: 1979 **Founders:** David Hummer and Randolph Ware
Brewer: David Zuckerman **Flagship beers:** Hola Maria, Buffalo Gold, Hazed, Singletrack, Pulp Fusion, Mojo, Due East, Shake **Seasonals/ special releases:** Bump 'n' Rind, Cold Hop, Irish Blessing, Nothing too Fancy, Slope Style, Killer Penguin, The Dude series **Tours:** Sun through Fri, 2 p.m.; Sat 2 and 4 p.m.

B oulder Beer Company began way back in 1979, making it Colorado's first craft brewery and one of the nation's first 50. The founders were two University of Colorado professors, and the early adopters encountered plenty

of troubles at the start. The brewery even changed the original name from Boulder Brewing a few times—first to Boulder Beer, then to Rockies Brewing, and then back to Boulder Beer.

The brewery's most well-known creation, Hazed and Infused, is a true craft beer icon and now known as just **Hazed**. It started as a homebrew recipe that Boulder Beer's brewer Aaron Hickman took to brewmaster David Zuckerman with the idea of making the bold dry-hopped amber ale professionally. Within 12 months, the hoppy session ale became the brewery's best-selling beer. More bold creations followed, including **Killer Penguin**, an American barleywine, and **Mojo IPA**, both mainstays of Boulder Beer's lineup to this day.

The brewery operates a popular taproom and full-service restaurant, better known to locals as Wilderness Pub, in a Boulder business park near the Flatirons. It hosts live music in the summer months, the patio is dog-friendly, and tours are offered regularly. Boulder Beer opened a new brewpub location downtown in the former Walnut Brewery space in 2017. The seven-barrel brewing system makes small batch beers that you can find only at the Walnut Street location, and it's open late for those college-town beer crawls.

Beer Lover's Pick

KILLER PENGUIN

Style: American Barleywine
ABV: 10 percent
Availability: Nov through Dec in bottles, bombers, and draft

Killer Penguin is an aggressive take on an aggressive style of beer, the hulking and sometimes intimidating American barleywine. Pouring a rusty color, the beer effervesces a thick, sugarcoated, pine-needle aroma. This big, 10 percent ABV monster has a palate-enveloping scorched caramel and bitter, dark-green herbaceous notes. The finish is boozy and bittersweet. The 22-ounce bottles are handsomely packaged with wax-sealed caps. This is a beer designed as much for cellaring to enjoy at a much later date as it is for drinking fresh.

SANITAS BREWING COMPANY

3550 Frontier Ave., Unit A, Boulder, CO 80301; (303) 442-4130; SanitasBrewing.com
Founded: 2013 **Founders:** Chris Coyne and Michael Memsic
Brewer: Chris Coyne **Flagship beers:** Saison, IPA, Hoppy Lager
Seasonals/special releases: Cherry Saison, Experimental Hop series, Deluge series, Train Beer series, Black IPA **Tours:** Sun through Fri, 2 p.m.; Sat 2 and 4 p.m. **Tours:** On request

A huge deck and backyard with a fire pit, games, lounge chairs, and taco truck make Sanitas Brewing the adult playground in Boulder. In the evenings, just visible over the trees, the sun sets behind the ridgeline that includes Mount Sanitas, and every now and then, a freight train rumbles by on the tracks that border the warehouse row where the brewery is located. The chill scene, from the well-appointed taproom to the outdoor companies in neighboring buildings, is hashtag Boulder.

The idea for the owl in the logo came to Chris Coyne and Michael Memsic, two former Boulder Beer brewers, as they planned Sanitas, making test batches late into the night. More than once, they would see an owl watching from above, and the bird became a patron saint of sorts for their beer. The logo also includes a six-pointed brewer's star like the ones used by breweries in Germany.

BLACK IPA

Style: Black IPA
ABV: 6.5 percent
Availability: On tap each fall and in cans

Sanitas once made the Black IPA year-round, and it's the first beer the brewery ever canned. The move toward lighter and fruiter IPAs pushed this one to the back burner, but each fall it returns. The beer pours straight black with a thick creamy khaki-colored head. But the cascade, centennial, and CTZ hops keep it bright and balanced, a perfect transition between summer IPAs and winter stouts.

Sanitas's flagship beer and one of its most popular is **Saison**. The light-bodied, estery beer is easily overlooked, but Sanitas takes pride in the fact that it became the first in the state to distribute the style in cans. The yeast gives it almost a bubble gum aroma, but it remains smooth on the finish. The brewery offers a dozen or so beers on tap, and a handful are experimental, such as a rotating hop series. Most of the beers pair well with McDevitt Taco Supply, a food trailer that is permanently parked at Sanitas and serves whenever the brewery is open. And if you're lucky enough to be there when the locomotive goes by, a special train beer is half price for the next 15 minutes.

UPSLOPE BREWING COMPANY

Flatiron Park; 1501 Lee Hill Rd., Boulder, CO 80304; (303) 449-2911; UpslopeBrewing.com; Taproom hours: Mon through Sun, 11 a.m. to 10 p.m.
Lee Hill; 1898 S. Flatiron Ct., Boulder, CO; (303) 396-1898; Taproom hours: Mon through Sun, 2 to 10 p.m.
Founded: 2008 **Founders:** Matt Cutter, Henry Wood, and Dany Pages **Brewers:** Alex Violette and Sam Scruby **Flagship beers:** India Pale Ale, Citra Pale Ale, Craft Lager, Experimental India Pale Ale, Rocky Mountain Kölsch **Seasonals/special releases:** Rocky Mountain Kölsch, Oatmeal Stout, Belgian Style Pale Ale, Thai Style White IPA, Pumpkin Ale, Blood Orange Saison, Christmas Ale, Lee Hill series,

Taproom series **Tours:** Sat, 4 to 5 p.m., at Lee Hill brewery. Sat, 3 p.m., at Flatiron Park location.

From the outset, founder Matt Cutter wanted to build a brewery that appealed to active, outdoorsy people who are socially and environmentally conscious like himself. The brewery chose to package only in cans—then a more rare idea but now common—to reduce the environmental impact. Upslope's delivery van was chosen because it is powered by natural gas, and the brewery is designed to use less water. The company is now a certified B corporation, emphasizing its social enterprise by donating to outdoor and environmental causes.

The outdoors mind-set is evident on the brewery's slogan, which proclaims, "Apres everything." The idea is to celebrate with beer all the time. The Tap Room series beers come in 19-ounce cans designed with a topographical map, a great look. And a number of the beers are ready-made for the summit, whether the crisp **Craft Lager** or the easy-drinking **Citra Pale Ale**. And the brewery makes one of Colorado's most coveted Pumpkin beers, which took top honors at GABF. The brewers bypassed the usual addition of huge pumpkin pie spices and instead just brewed with a mountain of pumpkin flesh.

The brewery operates two locations now. Lee Hill is the original one, where much of the experimental beer making takes place, while the location in Flatiron Park handles the big-production duties. The Lee Hill and Tap Room series beers are limited, creative one-offs from the production team.

FATE BREWING COMPANY

1600 38th St., Boulder, CO 80301; (303) 449-3283; Fate BrewingCompany.com
Founded: 2013 **Founder:** Mike Lawinski **Brewers:** Denise Jones, Jeff Griffith, and Josh Nard **Flagship beers:** Laimas Kölsch Style Ale, Parcae Belgian Style Pale Ale, Norns Roggenbier, Moirai India Pale Ale, Sudice American Stout **Seasonals/special releases:** Laimas Coffee Kölsch, Moirai Coffee IPA, Tequila Barrel Aged Uror Gose, Apollo Tsai, Barrel Aged Atropos Imperial IPA, Laimas Watermelon Kölsch Style Ale, Barrel Aged Clotho Cascadian Dark Ale **Tours:** Sun, 4 p.m., at Boulder location **Taproom hours:** Mon through Fri, 11 a.m. to 10 p.m.; Sat and Sun, 10 a.m. to 10 p.m.

Founder Mike Lawinski spent a decade working at other Boulder restaurants and calls it his fate to open his own place. Fate distributes across the state, and the brewpub in Boulder features 30 taps, a handful of which are guest beers from other breweries. The fate theme extends to the beer names, and the beer theme extends to the menu.

The core beers take a retro approach—a light beer, a pale ale, a red ale, an IPA, and a dark beer—but others on the tap list get more creative.

The award-winning **Laimas Kölsch-style Ale** (pronounced "ly-muhs") is a reference to Baltic mythology and the three goddesses that determined fate. Light golden in color, the beer hits the style marks with a touch of hops, a hint of malt sweetness, and a refreshing, crisp finish. The **Sudice American Stout** pulls from a tale of destiny in Slavic mythology. It pours dark with a big roasted malt flavor and a surprising punch of citrus hops on the end. The **Uror Gose** is a German-style wheat sour with coriander and sea salt, a quenching combination that keeps you sipping. The version aged in tequila barrels only makes it more interesting.

The food helps set Fate apart from many other brewpubs. From healthy and seasonal to barbecue that is smoked daily, the menu offers different takes on traditional plates. On the brunch menu, you'll find a seasonal beer pancake that, like the taps, rotates frequently.

MOUNTAIN SUN PUB & BREWERY

1535 Pearl St., Boulder, CO 80302; (303) 546-0886; MountainSunPub.com; Taproom hours: Mon through Sun, 11 to 1 a.m.
Southern Sun Pub & Brewery; 627 S. Broadway, Boulder, CO 80305; (303) 543-0886; Taproom hours: Mon through Fri, 11:30 to 1 a.m.; Sat and Sun, 11 to 1 a.m.
Vine Street Pub & Brewery; 1700 Vine St., Denver, CO 80206; (303) 388-2337; Taproom hours: Mon through Sun, 11 to 1 a.m.
Founded: 1993 **Founder:** Kevin Daly **Brewers:** John Fiorilli and Davis Brown **Flagship beers:** Big Krane Kölsch, Number One Belgian Tripel, Blackberry Wheat, Colorado Kind Ale, Isadore Java Porter, FYIPA, Illusion Dweller IPA, XXX Pale Ale, Annapurna Amber **Seasonals/special releases:** Prime Time Pilsner, Franklin's Strong Golden, Soul Flower Saison, White Fawn Hoppy Wheat, Hop Vivant Imperial IPA, Pearl Street Porter, Yonder Mountain Stout, Korova Cream Stout, Oatimus Prime Imperial Stout **Tours:** On request. Growlers to go at Southern Sun and Vine Street.

E ven with three locations, Mountain Sun is not a typical brewpub chain. The original Mountain Sun location on Boulder's bustling Pearl Street first fired its brew kettle in 1993. Colorful murals and Grateful Dead posters line the walls, and 20 taps of mostly house-brewed beer flow daily until 1 a.m., a nod to its college-town digs.

The second location, Southern Sun, opened in 2002 south of Boulder, a location that means that the crowd is more family oriented. In 2008, Mountain Sun's third location, Vine Street, opened for business in Denver's Uptown neighborhood as a mellow hangout. All are a bit of a throwback without TVs, and none take credit cards (cash or check only). The owners also operate two beer pubs: Under the Sun Eatery & Pizzeria downstairs in the same building as Southern Sun and Longs Peak Pub in Longmont.

All the beer is brewed at Southern Sun and Vine Street with the nine core brands available at each location. These include **Colorado Kind Ale**, a 6.3 percent ABV American amber ale with a thick, leafy-green, medium-bitter hop profile and a solid-malt base, and **FYIPA**, a big, 7.2 percent ABV hop monster that packs bright-yellow citrus and tropical fruit notes with notes of eucalyptus and mango.

The rest of the beer menu rotates often with 124 beers posted in one recent year. The time to visit is February for the popular Stout Month. Well in advance, the brewers from each Mountain Sun location get together to brainstorm new and different stouts. The brew ingredient list includes the likes of tangerine, coffee, chai spices, chili, cherry, chocolate, and mint.

On the food side, the brewpubs offer menus with wide varieties of both vegetarian- and meat-focused staples that include daily varieties of fresh hummus, exotic grilled-cheese sandwiches, a tempeh Reuben, and a vast selection of burgers, and veggie burgers.

TWISTED PINE BREWING COMPANY

3201 Walnut St., Suite A, Boulder, CO 80301; (303) 786-9270; TwistedPineBrewing.com
Founded: 1995 **Founder:** Gordon Knight **Brewer:** Bob Baile
Flagship beers: Hoppy Boy India Pale Ale, American Amber Ale, Honey Brown, Cream Style Stout, Rocky Mountain Wheat, Billy's Chilies, Big Shot Espresso Stout, Ghost Face Killah **Seasonals/special releases:** Blond Ale, Raspberry Wheat, Pearl Street Porter, Reilly's Oak Whiskey Red, Northstar Imperial Porter, Hoppy Man, Le Petit Saison, Razzy Xpress
Tours: None **Taproom hours:** Mon through Sun, 11 a.m. to 10 p.m.

Boulder's Twisted Pine is the second of three breweries founded by Colorado brewing legend and entrepreneur Gordon Knight. It started the opposite of most, focusing first on production and distribution and then adding a tasting room and a restaurant that gives it a more brewpub vibe now. It's become a staple of the Boulder beer scene.

The taproom features as many as 24 beers and offers a wide selection of the brewery's year-round beers, seasonals, special releases, and one-off experiments, the latter thanks to a small-batch system that allows brewers to get creative. In many ways, experiments define Twisted Pine. From a handful of different IPAs to a braggot, little, if anything, seems off-limits. That ethos has carried over into the brewery's production beers, too.

Beer Lover's Pick

GHOST FACE KILLAH

Style: Chili Beer
ABV: 5 percent
Availability: Limited release

Even if this is not everyone's favorite beer, it's almost a rite of passage. The idea for an even spicier incarnation of Billy's Chilies was seeded at a festival in 2009 when a brazen attendee suggested that Twisted Pine could make an even hotter version. Not one to shy away, the brewers emerged with a beer brewed with the addition of one of the hottest peppers, the so-called ghost pepper, or Bhut Jolokia. The beer is aimed squarely at the more adventurous drinker.

Billy's Chilies is a light, 5 percent ABV wheat beer infused with a tea made from serrano, habanero, jalapeño, Anaheim, and Fresno chili peppers. The resulting beer has a bright-green, bell-pepper aroma and a multifaceted peppery flavor. Layers of heat and red-vegetal flavor give way to a clean, refreshing finish.

Big Shot Espresso Stout is a hefty American stout conditioned on significant quantities of espresso coffee. Drinking the beer is something akin to enjoying a strong iced coffee. Heavily roasted bitterness and chocolate-covered coffee-bean flavors persist to the finish. **Le Petit Saison** is an unexpected Belgian-style beer among Twisted Pine's extensive range of American standard and experimental ales. Le Petit is a classic saison, or farmhouse ale, with a woolly nose and sweet fruity body. Bitterness is minimal and the finish gentle.

BACKCOUNTRY PIZZA & TAP HOUSE

2319 Arapahoe Ave., Boulder, CO 80302; (303) 449-4285;
BackcountryPizzaAndTapHouse.info
Taps: 68+ **Bottles/cans:** 300+

The beer list here is nothing short of stunning. And that's why Backcountry Pizza & Tap House in Boulder is one of the best beer bars in the nation.

The tough part is deciding what beer to drink from a menu with 68 taps, two casks, and a book-length bottle list numbering north of 300 beers from across the globe. **Tip:** Order a few five-ounce pours to try a variety in one style and sip while you peruse the bottle list and calculate whether you have the money to splurge because this is definitely the place to try some of the rarer beers poured anywhere in America, including limited-release domestic and international sour and barrel-aged beers as well as IPAs from Europe, New Zealand, and beyond. The draft list includes plenty of Colorado breweries in each style category, such as Crooked Stave, WeldWerks, and TRVE.

The restaurant's main features are pizzas and calzones, so try the Mt. Hawaiian or Mr. Pesto. Elsewhere on the menu, you'll find soups and salads, appetizers like waffle fries and wings, and plenty of sandwiches and burgers.

RUEBEN'S BURGER BISTRO

1800 Broadway St., Boulder, CO 80302; (303) 443-5000;
RuebensBurgerBistro.com
Taps: 44 **Bottles/cans:** 300+

Rueben's is one of Boulder's top burger joints with 15 different options on the menu and a make-your-own route if you can't find what you want to satisfy the craving. The burgers are served on a pretzel bun that sops up the juices. And because they think so highly of their burgers, they pledge to serve them with "the best beer in the world."

The hyperbole aside, Rueben's is unapologetic about what it considers the "best beer"—Belgians. The menu is 18 pages long, and dubbels, tripels, and quadrupels dominate the space. There's even more—much more—on a bottle list that will consume you with its variety and options. The dedication means that brands like Rochefort, La Trappe, Westmalle, and Chimay color the menu. Whether Belgians are old or current favorites, the variety is well displayed on the list and extends to sours.

The second-best beer, the restaurant claims, is Colorado beer. So the menu includes a number of local brews, covering all style categories and extending to the eight rotating taps. If you're having trouble making a decision, the staff can offer its favorites on the menu, which is helpful for calibrating your taste buds.

THE WEST END TAVERN

**926 Pearl St., Boulder, CO 80302; (303) 444-3535; TheWestEndTavern.com
Taps:** 25 **Bottles/cans:** 20+

The West End Tavern is located on Boulder's Pearl Street Mall in a district of elevated retail shops and restaurants. The tavern does everything right, from the carefully curated tap selections to its bottle list and well-prepared food. Each July, West End hosts a minifestival featuring "the biggest and baddest" IPAs from different breweries across the country, an event that showcases the place's beer prowess.

West End is a part of the Big Red F Restaurant Group, which also owns Jax Fish House in Boulder, Denver, and Fort Collins; Zolo Grill; Centro Mexican Kitchen; and Lola, all highly rated local eateries. In addition to the 25 nicely curated beer taps, which often include pilot batches from local breweries and hard-to-find imports, the tavern also prides itself on a menu of more than 75 bourbons. The bartenders also can whip up a delicious beer cocktail if you ask politely. Diners and drinkers can sit downstairs at the bar and get some beer or bourbon schooling from the knowledgeable staff or get comfy at one of the adjacent booth-style tables. Better yet, go upstairs to the heated roof terrace, which has its own bar and service.

For food, highlights include cornbread skillet, wings, house-smoked pork ribs, picnic eggs, and a roster of smoked meats, including brisket, pulled pork, and ribs.

Fort Collins

The prominence of Fort Collins as a beer city belies the fact it remained dry until 1969. It took a movement led by students at Colorado State University to allow more than the sale of 3.2 beer. The first brewery came two decades later when Anheuser-Busch pioneered a change in local laws and built a massive plant along the interstate outside the downtown district. Soon after, two craft brewers, Odell and New Belgium, would begin operations and start a transformation that made it the state's beer hub for decades. Odell and New Belgium helped spawn countless smaller operations and now boast massive destination breweries that rank at the top of the must-visit list. It's hard to understate the connection between New Belgium's national brand and Colorado's place on the beer map. Even if Denver now outpaces Fort Collins when it comes to the brewing scene, the small city still offers a dense concentration of breweries. It's a great place to get a sense of the state's laid-back beer vibe and see how stalwarts of the industry continue to redefine the craft beer industry. And true to the New Belgium brand, a bike tour is a great way to do it.

ANHEUSER-BUSCH BREWING COMPANY, FORT COLLINS BREWERY

2351 Busch Dr., Fort Collins, CO 80524; (970) 490-4691; Anheuser-Busch.com
Founded: 1988 **Founder:** Adolphus Busch **Brewers:** Various
Flagship beers: Budweiser, Bud Light, Bud Light Platinum, Bud Light Lime, Budweiser Select, Bud Ice, Michelob, Michelob Light, Michelob ULTRA, AmberBock, Busch, Busch Light, Natural Light, Natural Ice, O'Doul's, O'Doul's Amber, Landshark, Shock Top, Rolling Rock, Goose Island 312, Goose Island IPA and Goose Island Honkers Ale **Seasonals/ special releases:** Shock Top Raspberry, Shock Top Pumpkin Wheat, Michelob Pumpkin Spice Ale and more **Tours:** Mon, 11 a.m. to 4 p.m.; Thurs to Sun, 11 a.m. to 4 p.m. **Taproom hours:** Sun and Mon, 11 a.m. to 6 p.m.; Wed and Thurs, 11 a.m. to 4 p.m.; Fri and Sat, 11 a.m. to 8 p.m.

Colorado has such a widespread reputation as a craft beer capital that many are surprised to learn that the third-oldest operating brewery in the state is actually the Anheuser-Busch facility in Fort Collins, which came online in 1988.

The scale of brewing undertaken at Anheuser-Busch is truly breathtaking with the total floor area at 1 million square feet. The property is 1,130 acres and includes research facilities in a small building within sight of the brewery. Constructed on a rail line with direct access to I-25, the brewery was purposely positioned to deliver fresh beer to the Rocky Mountain region, West Coast, and Midwest as quickly as possible. It operates around the clock, seven days a week, brewing nearly 30 different beers, including the various Michelob and Shock Top brands, as well as former craft brewers, such as Goose Island. In keeping with Colorado's position as a pioneering beer state, beers like Shock Top Belgian White and others were developed at the Fort Collins brewery before being rolled out nationally.

Nearly 100,000 people visit the brewery every year. The tours are informative and deliver a surprisingly up-close and personal experience that ends at the *biergarten* and views of the mountains. One of the highlights of the tour is a visit to the stables, where the West Coast display team of Anheuser-Busch's famous Clydesdale horses lives.

FUNKWERKS

1900 E. Lincoln Ave., Unit B, Fort Collins, CO 80524; (970) 482-3865; Funkwerks.com
Founded: 2010 **Founders:** Gordon Schuck and Brad Lincoln
Brewers: Gordon Schuck and Brad Lincoln **Flagship beers:** Saison, Tropic King, Raspberry Provincial, Pineapple Provincial **Seasonals/ special releases:** Dark Prophet, Quad, Oud Bruin, Peachy King, Bramble, Saison d'Brett **Tours:** Fri and Sat, 2 p.m., 3 p.m., and 4 p.m. **Taproom hours:** Sun through Thurs, 11 a.m. to 8 p.m.; Fri and Sat, 11 a.m. to 9 p.m. Growlers and bottles to go.

Gordon Schuck and Brad Lincoln came from different backgrounds. Schuck made a mark as an award-winning homebrewer. Lincoln worked as an accountant with a passion for craft beer on the side. The two met in the brewing science program at the Siebel Institute of Technology in Chicago, and once they graduated, they opened Funkwerks as a saison-focused brewery.

Saisons—French for "season"—originated from the French-speaking region of Belgium and once were the drink of seasonal farm laborers. The easy-drinking style is a gateway for many newcomers to craft beer, and Funkwerks makes some of the best. The brewery won the Small Brewing Company of the Year award at the GABF in 2012 and grew quickly into one of Colorado's great niche breweries, expanding from one barrel to 160 in five years. The brewery is now part of a team with 21st Amendment and Brooklyn Brewery after the latter took a minority interest in the two smaller operations to help them grow.

Fort Collins

Beer Lover's Pick

TROPIC KING

Style: Imperial Saison
ABV: 8 percent
Availability: Year-round on tap and in bottles
Brewed with a New Zealand hops, Tropic King is a higher-ABV saison with lots of tropical fruit aroma and flavor. The nose is ablaze with notes of peach, mango, sweet peppers, and fresh ginger. The same follows for the flavor, with strong yeast-derived fruity and pepper notes and a less-dry-than-expected finish. The big flavor and loyal following is amusing given that the beer started as an accident after extra bags of Munich malt were added to the brew.

The **Saison** is a good place to start a tasting flight. The beer started as Schuck's homebrew recipe and now is considered one of the best in its class with aromas and flavors of passion fruit and tangerine from the yeast esters and a dry finish. There is a refreshing brilliance to the drink, sip through swallow.

HORSE & DRAGON BREWING COMPANY

124 Racquette Dr., Fort Collins, CO 80524; (970) 631-8038; HorseAndDragonBrewing.com
Founded: 2014 **Founders:** Tim and Carol Cochran **Brewers:** Josh Evans and Titus Bentley **Flagship beers:** NoCo, Sad Panda **Seasonals/special releases:** H&D, Almost Summer, N+1, Harry Hughes's Aggie Ale, Agitated Aardvark, Picnic Rock **Tours:** Sat and Sun, 12:30 p.m. **Taproom hours:** Mon through Sun, noon to 6 p.m. Growlers to go.

The first desire for opening a brewery came to Tim and Carol Cochran on their honeymoon in Napa Valley, California, where, instead of drinking wine, they spent a good bit of time at local brewpubs. It took many years, but the couple eventually found their place in Fort Collins, where they had family.

Horse & Dragon is located in a former airplane hangar in an industrial park north of downtown. The brewery celebrates its environmental stewardship

efforts, offsetting all its energy usage with wind power and reducing greenhouse gas emissions. The brewery's name is derived from the Chinese Zodiac, and the artwork is Asian inspired. (The actual planning for the brewery began in January 2013 at the end of the Year of the Dragon, and the place opened in the Year of the Horse.) Tim Cochran worked for Miller Brewing and made beer at home for years, but when it came time to open his own operation, he hired Linsey Cornish from Odell Brewing, the city's only female head brewer at one point.

Cornish later left, but she developed the beer that Horse & Dragon is best known for, **Sad Panda**, a rich but drinkable coffee stout. The rest of the beer menu shows a dedication to nuanced flavors from malts and fruit additions,

SAD PANDA

Style: Coffee Stout
ABV: 6.8 percent
Availability: Year-round on tap

Far too often, coffee stouts experience an identity crisis. Is the flavor profile a stout with coffee or coffee with stout? This is not the case with Sad Panda, an example with enough balance to show the flavors of the beer and the coffee. The sweetness from the vanilla and the chocolate flavors blend well with the bitterness of the coffee. It pours dark with a tan head that misleads about its drinkability.

whether it's a nitro honey brown ale or a pineapple ginger lager. A least a dozen beers are on tap at any given time, so it's a good place to experiment with new flavors and styles in a flight.

JESSUP FARM BARREL HOUSE

1921 Jessup Dr., Fort Collins, CO 80525; (970) 568-8345; JessupFarmBarrelHouse.com
Founded: 2015 **Founders:** Jeff Albarella, Gordon Schuck, and Brad Lincoln **Brewer:** Jeff Albarella **Flagship beers:** Wood Knot, Hurry Up and Wait, Helles in Wonderland, Train Delay **Seasonals/special releases:** Fancy Pants, UB Funky, Unicorn Bubbles, Field to Peel, Feats of Strength, Legal in Europe, Jimmy Buffett Problem **Tours:** On request **Taproom hours:** Mon through Thurs, 11 a.m. to 9 p.m.; Fri and Sat, 11 a.m. to 11 p.m.; Sun, 11 a.m. to 9 p.m. Bottles and growlers to go

Jessup Farm Barrel House makes beer that befits its home. Located in a 133-year-old restored barn as part of a re-created farmstead village, the brewery makes only barrel-aged beers, as in the Old World. The first floor is used for fermenting beer, and the taproom is located upstairs in what would have been the hayloft, where people now sit at a long bar and communal tables surrounded by barrels and exposed rafters.

The niche fits well for Jessup Farm Barrel House, which is an offshoot of Funkwerks and shares two of the same founders. The beer is actually brewed at Funkwerks and transferred to the barn, where it is fermented and blended in barrels. The process allows Jessup Farm to split batches and experiment.

What brewer Jeff Albarella hopes to showcase is nuanced barrel-aged beer, not the big, boozy, huge beers that are so often associated with the category. Most of Jessup Farm's beers are lower in alcohol, and Albarella hopes that the approachability makes it appealing to a wider audience. A good example is the award-winning **Fancy Pants**, an IPA with *Brettanomyces* that is dry-hopped and aged in oak barrels.

None of this is to say that the beer is boring by any stretch. The barrels used include Scotch, tequila, gin, and wine varieties. **Jimmy Buffett Problem** is a pineapple and coconut double IPA aged in a blend of first-fill rum and second-fill bourbon barrels. And **Legal in Europe** is the base **Feats of Strength** stout with a kick of chiles, chocolate, and cinnamon aged in whiskey barrels. The brewery also boasts a large outdoor patio and a small menu with bites to eat or chocolate and beer pairings.

NEW BELGIUM BREWING COMPANY

500 Linden St., Fort Collins, CO 80524; (970) 221-0524; NewBelgium.com; Taproom hours: Mon through Sun, 11 a.m. to 8 p.m.
The Woods By New Belgium; 3350 Brighton Blvd., Denver, CO 80216; Taproom hours: Sun through Wed, 6 a.m. to 11 p.m.; Thurs through Sat, 6 to 2 a.m.
Founded: 1991 **Founders:** Jeff Lebesch and Kim Jordan **Brewer:** Christian Holbrook **Flagship beers:** Fat Tire, Citradelic, Dayblazer, Old Aggie, Pilsener, The Hemperor, Mural, Voodoo Ranger, Voodoo Ranger Juicy Haze **Seasonals/special releases:** Voodoo Ranger Imperial, Voodoo Ranger 8 Hop, Voodoo Ranger Liquid Paradise, Voodoo Ranger Guava Spruce, Voodoo Ranger Atomic Pumpkin Ale, Fat Tire Belgian White, Abbey, Trippel, 1554, Tartastic Lemon Ginger, Tartastic Strawberry Lemon, La Folie, Le Terroir, Transatlantique Kriek **Tours:** Mon through Sun, every hour from 11:30 a.m. to 4:30 p.m. in Fort Collins. Book

reservations months in advance, as tours are popular. Growlers, bottles, and cans to go at the Fort Collins location.

In 1986, homebrewer, electrical engineer, and future New Belgium Brewing Company cofounder Jeff Lebesch was riding his mountain bike through Belgium when he had a beer epiphany at a bar called Brugge Beertje. On that day, the breadth and dynamic nature of Belgian beers changed his perception of beer for good. On his return to the US, Jeff brewed an abbey-style ale and an amber ale called Fat Tire in honor of his life-changing journey on bike. The rest, to put it mildly, is history.

Fat Tire is New Belgium's flagship beer and endures as a perfect gateway beer for those migrating from lighter offerings. Drinking one fresh is a bucket list item for serious beer adventurers. And New Belgium's massive and ever-expanding brewery provides a great backdrop. The Fort Collins location offers 90-minute tours, a wide-open lawn for sipping and games, and a huge taproom with multiple bars that serve beers available only on-site. If you visit one brewery or join one tour in Colorado, this is the one to take. More recently, New Belgium opened a small pilot brewery and rooftop bar dubbed The Woods at The Source Hotel in Denver, where it will highlight small-batch beers.

The brewer behind the original sour program—one of the first and most robust in the US—is Peter Bouckaert, who left the company in 2017 to start his own venture, Purpose Brewing and Cellars. New Belgium continues to keep current on the latest trends, even making forays into extending its reach with the **Dayblazer** and **Mural**, two beers designed to compete with mass-market

Beer Lover's Pick

LA FOLIE

Style: Flanders-style sour brown ale
ABV: 7 percent
Availability: On draft year-round and in bottles
Considered the first commercial sour beer to be released by a US craft brewery, New Belgium's La Folie is a Flanders-style sour brown aged in oak barrels that delivers a puckering tartness. The color is rich and masks a sharp Lambic sourness that is an acquired taste. Once you do, though, the complexity of the flavors opens up with dark fruit and bright-ness with sweet threads and a smoothness.

offerings from the megabrewers. At the same time, the brewery is doubling down on higher-end offerings, whether more sour variations or the hop-forward **Voodoo Ranger** series.

ODELL BREWING COMPANY

800 E. Lincoln Ave., Fort Collins, CO 80524; (970) 498-9070; OdellBrewing.com; Taproom hours: Mon through Thurs, 11 a.m. to 6 p.m.; Fri through Sat, 11 a.m. to 7 p.m.
2945 Larimer St., Denver, CO 80205; (720) 795-7862; Taproom hours: Sun through Tues, noon to 10 p.m.; Wed through Sat, noon to midnight
Founded: 1989 **Founder:** Doug Odell **Brewer:** Brendan McGivney
Flagship beers: Colorado Lager, 90 Shilling Ale, Sippin Pretty, IPA, Myrcenary, Drumroll, Rupture, Easy Street Wheat, Cuthroat Porter, 5 Barrel Pale Ale, Levity Amber Ale, Loose Leaf **Seasonals/special releases:** St. Lupulin, Oktoberfest, Isolation Ale, Tree Shaker, Cloud Catcher, Friek, Fee Fi Fo Fum, Jolly Russian **Tours:** Mon through Sat, 1 p.m., 2 p.m., and 3 p.m. Growlers, crowlers, cans, and bottled beers to go at the Fort Collins location.

Founded in 1989 by Doug Odell, Odell Brewing is one of the oldest breweries in Colorado—but it doesn't act its age. Whereas other early adapters like New Belgium exploded in size and made a national footprint, Odell is committed to slow growth and distributed to only 18 states in 2018.

IPA

Style: IPA

ABV: 7 percent

Availability: Year-round on draft and in bottles and cans

Odell Brewing uses pale and Vienna malts—in combination with nine different US hop varieties—to make one of the standard-bearing beers in the IPA category. It hits all the high marks with a crisp, strong bitterness; a malt profile that is substantive but not sweet; hop aromatics and flavors that add a dynamic flavor; and a 7 percent ABV that says fun without going too far. It's the go-to in any setting, whether a tailgate or dinner plate.

Odell Brewing Company

Fort Collins

The company built a new state-of-the-art brewery in 2010 that focuses on sustainability when it comes to saving energy and water. But the first thing visitors will notice is the huge patio and yard off the taproom, a place so inviting in the warmer months that as long as the beer flows, you won't want to leave. The real prize is located inside the brew house, where a small-batch system lets Odell Brewing continue to innovate and adapt to new flavor trends faster than most breweries. All the beers that are packaged to sell started on the pilot system before entering larger production.

Odell released an opaque pale ale called **Drumroll** to the Colorado market before most breweries tapped into the hazy IPA trends, and it even distributed a creamsicle and peach–flavored milkshake IPA called **Cloud Catcher**. Other innovations include **Sippin Pretty**, a low-alcohol fruited sour series in a can, and the Cellar Series, which features 12-ounce bottles of limited beers, such as barrel-aged brews that often rotate.

One of Odell's top new beers is **Rupture**, a pale ale where whole cone hops are ground in a hammer mill and tossed in the brew, a process that is akin to fresh ground beans in coffee. But the brewery still makes its name on **90 Shilling** and **IPA**, two mainstays whose tastes continue to endure as landmarks in their respective styles.

The most recent adventure for Odell is a new taproom and pilot brewery in Denver. The RiNo brewery offers beers that you can find only on-site.

PURPOSE BREWING & CELLARS

4025 S. Mason St., Unit C, Fort Collins, CO 80525; (970) 377-4107; PurposeBrewing.com
Founded: 2017 **Founders:** Peter and Frezi Bouckaert and Laura and Zach Wilson **Brewers:** Peter Bouckaert and Zach Wilson **Flagship beers:** None **Seasonals/special releases:** Smoeltrekker **Tours:** On request **Taproom hours:** Thurs, 3 to 7 p.m.; Fri through Sun, noon to 7 p.m.

Purpose Brewing & Cellars defies traditions. Most of its beer fits no particular style. Often the brews feature interesting ingredients. And the brewery never makes the same beer more than once, meaning that each time you visit during the limited hours, there's something new to try. You'll want to try them all, too.

The brewer behind Purpose is Peter Bouckaert, the former brewmaster at New Belgium Brewing who previously worked for a decade at Brewery Rodenbach. He's a sour beer master and a published author on the topic. He partnered with Zach Wilson, who worked for 1933 Brewing Company, to create the new operation. It's located in the same space as Wilson's old brewery south of downtown Fort Collins. What the two do is essentially play with beer and let their creativity take them in new directions, even if it's wacky and weird. One example from a recent menu is a sour blonde made with a mixed culture and Szechuan peppercorns and then dry-hopped with mosaic hops. The four-barrel brew house fits the small-batch niche, and the 70 barrels allow for various blending and lengthy cellar times.

The brewery has only four taps and tries to keep a barrel-aged brew on the menu at all times. Every now and then, you'll find a traditional beer, like a recent stout brewed with local malt. One beer the brewery keeps making—but in different variations—is **Smoeltrekker**, which in Flemish means "to put on a funny face," much like you'd do if you tasted a sour beer. Overall, the experience is definitely aimed at the adventurous or experienced craft beer fan.

COOPERSMITH'S PUB AND BREWERY

5 Old Town Sq., Fort Collins, CO 80524; (970) 498-0483;
CooperSmithsPub.com
Founded: 1989 **Founders:** Scott Smith and Brad Page **Brewer:**
Dwight Hall **Flagship beers:** Allber damn bitter, Nut Brown Ale,
Horsetooth Stout, Poudre Pale Ale, Punjabi Pale Ale, Sigda's Green Chile
Seasonals/special releases: Kriek, Blood Orange Wheat, What-A-
Melon **Tours:** By appointment **Taproom hours:** Sun through Thurs,
11 a.m. to 10 p.m.; Fri and Sat, 11 a.m. to 11 p.m. Growlers to go.

CooperSmith's Pub and Brewery opened in Old Town Fort Collins in 1989, the year after Wynkoop opened for business in a dilapidated downtown Denver neighborhood. CooperSmith's founders, Scott Smith and Brad Page, had looked to Wynkoop's owners for help with their business plan before pulling the trigger on their own brewpub. And like their forefather, Scott and Brad eventually found themselves at the heart of the revival of Old Town Fort Collins.

The brewery and restaurant were constructed in an old grocery store in the heart of the college town. Today, the brewery feels so at home that you might assume that CooperSmith's had occupied the location for 100 years.

Now an institution, CooperSmith's, of course, has its staple beers. One of the boldest is **Sigda's Green Chile** ale, which is thought to be the first year-round chili beer served anywhere in the country. The 5.4 percent ABV golden pour is brewed with Anaheim and serrano chilies, and rather than burning the palate with pepper-derived heat, it delivers a pleasant and breezy vegetal freshness.

Over the course of a year, CooperSmith's brews and serves nearly 70 different beers, with styles running the gamut from Belgian sours to seldom-brewed, cask-conditioned English styles served from a traditional hand pump.

CooperSmith's is divided into two sides: the Pubside and the Poolside. The Pubside menu offers up an extremely wide and encompassing selection of British-, American-, and Mexican-inspired pub fare, from burgers and fish-and-chips to pastas and brick-oven pizzas. The Poolside offers up more American bar classics, with a greater emphasis on burgers, pizzas, wings, nachos, and the like. And the Poolside, which features billiards, is open late for the college crowd.

CHOICE CITY BUTCHER & DELI

104 W. Olive St., Fort Collins, CO 80524; (970) 490-2489;
ChoiceCityButcher.com
Taps: 37 **Bottles/cans:** 20+

Choice City Butcher & Deli, named from a moniker for Fort Collins, is probably one of the few craft beer–centric New York–style delicatessens in America. No surprise, then, that this excellent and well-executed concept has been rated in years past as one of the best beer restaurants in America.

Behind the register, the wall is lined with nearly 40 taps, pouring the likes of hard-to-find imports; rare, barrel-aged American offerings; and small one-off batch beers by local Colorado breweries. In addition to the jaw-dropping tap list, Choice City also has a bottle list of intriguing and often limited-release beers.

In terms of food, Choice City is a butcher as well as a restaurant and, as such, is a true meat lovers' Valhalla. The breakfast menu includes corned beef or buffalo hash with eggs, savory stuffed crepes, eggs Benedict, and chicken-fried steak. For lunch, how about a Colorado buffalo Reuben, Italian multimeat sub, sausage sandwich, grilled cheese, or Philly cheesesteak? Dinner could include a buffalo chicken salad, buffalo meat and bacon sliders, rib eye crepes, or chile rellenos raviolis.

THE MAYOR OF OLD TOWN

632 S. Mason St., Fort Collins, CO 80524; (970) 682-2410;
TheMayorofOldTown.com
Taps: 100 **Bottles/cans:** 50

The Mayor of Old Town is one of Fort Collins's best places to go if you want to sample a lot of local, national, and international beers. The bar has an impressive array of 100 taps. While there are plenty of chain beer restaurants that boast a long list of beers, the offerings can stray toward generic. The Mayor is different. Here you will find special batches from local Fort Collins breweries—such as New Belgium's amazing **Blackberry Oscar** wild ale and rare barrel-aged beers from the East Coast and West Coast. The bar even collaborates with local breweries to make beers you can only find at The Mayor.

The owners put a focus on getting the best and most interesting beers out there, and one-third of the beer board is often imports. The quality imported beers from Belgium, Germany, the UK, and beyond include **Trappist Rochefort 6** and **Rochefort 8**.

It's an experience that spans the spectrum of beer drinkers, from newcomers to the beer nerds. The food menu at The Mayor is more upscale than in the past. It's still bar food, but you can get a blackened tuna sandwich in addition to those double-stacked burgers and parmesan truffle fries.

TAP AND HANDLE

307 S. College Ave., Fort Collins, CO 80524; (970) 484-1116; TapAndHandle.com
Taps: 74 **Bottles:** 100+

Tap and Handle speaks to Fort Collins's beer-loving sensibilities. First, it's located a couple doors down from Choice City Butcher & Deli in the Old Town, two great beers spots in one area. Second, it's owned by the publishers of *Craft Beer & Brewing* magazine, Kate Davis and Andrew Fitzgibbon. The two took over when Jeff Willis, a longtime mainstay in Colorado's craft beer scene, returned to Texas to open his own brewery.

A few years back, Tap and Handle was one of a handful of Colorado bars named in the top 100 in the nation. Fitzgibbon says the key to Tap and Handle's success is to keep relevant by tapping what's trending in the market and what consumers want to see. The 74 taps present an overwhelming dilemma for all, even the beer geeks this place draws. WeldWerks Brewing's **Juicy Bits**, a nationally sought-after hazy IPA, is essentially the house beer and usually on tap. And Bierstadt Lagerhaus makes the journey from Denver in the form of its great **Helles**. The huge tap list allows the bar to keep more than a dozen sour beers pouring at all times as well as at least one barrel-aged option.

The food menu is simple, but a smoker adds plenty of tasty options. The most popular menu item is the chicken fingers, which are made fresh all day long in a house beer batter.

Northern Front Range

Greeley, Idaho Springs, Lafayette, Longmont, and Loveland

Most of Colorado's best beer is situated in the northern Front Range, and the cities of Denver, Boulder and Fort Collins get the most attention. But dozens of smaller breweries are beginning to fill in the gaps between the populated craft beer havens and make names for themselves in the small cities that dot the northeastern quadrant of the state. This section includes two big names in the craft beer industry— Left Hand and Oskar Blues, which are as integral to the state's beer scene as New Belgium, Odell, and Great Divide. Most of the action is concentrated near I-25, which runs north to south through Colorado. But the region also extends west of the Denver area suburbs and into the mountains, where two breweries in Idaho Springs make for great pit stops along I-70 if you're headed to the ski resorts or hiking trails. The vast reach of good beer—and the diversity of the offerings—is just another attribute that elevates Colorado's brewing culture.

CELLAR WEST ARTISAN ALES

778 W. Baseline Rd., Unit B, Lafayette, CO; (720) 465-9346; CellarWest.com
Founded: 2016 **Founder:** Zach Nichols **Brewer:** Zach Nichols
Flagship beer: Westfield **Seasonal/special releases:** Sapience and Make Hay **Tours:** On request **Taproom hours:** Tues through Friday, 3 to 10 p.m.; Sat and Sun, 1 to 10 p.m. Bottles to go.

When Zach Nichols found himself at the beer store, he kept reaching for farmhouse ales and saisons only to realize that most were made by out-of-state brewers. He saw an opening for a new brewery in Colorado that focused on the styles and appealed to the local beer crowd. So the former Sanitas Brewing owner started Cellar West Artisan Ales in Boulder. He brewed at night at other area breweries and trucked the unfermented wort back to his place for fermentation and packaging.

He quickly found a market for the barrel-aged and mixed-culture beers. And before long, he moved into a larger space with its own brew house in

Lafayette, an emerging beer center. Cellar West specializes in Belgian-style farmhouse ales, and its house strain of wild yeast features a heavy dose of *Brettanomyces* to add the funky attributes to beer that Nichols kept searching for in the store. The brewery makes farmhouse IPAs but no clean versions of the style. Nichols added a secondary focus on lagers and hopes to have one or two on tap at all times. In a brewery with a constantly evolving bottle list, **Westfield** is as close as Cellar West comes to a flagship beer. It's a multigrain saison with wheat, barley, oats, and rye that comes across gold in color with an effervescent but full mouthfeel to complement herbal notes from the light dry hop of pekko hops.

GRIMM BROTHERS BREWHOUSE

623 N. Denver Ave., Loveland, CO 80538; (970) 624-6045; GrimmBrosBrewhouse.com
Founded: 2010 **Founders:** Don Chapman and Aaron Heaton **Brewer:** Laura Pilato **Flagship beers:** Snow Drop, Little Red Cap, Fearless Youth, The Griffin **Seasonals/special releases:** Farmers Daughter, Maiden's Kiss, The Baron series, Dragon's Bloom, True Bride **Tours:** By appointment **Taproom hours:** Mon through Thurs, 1 to 9 p.m.; Fri and Sat, noon to 9 p.m.; Sun, 1 to 7 p.m. Growlers and bottles to go.

In an effort to avoid opening a brewery that simply served yet another IPA and pale ale, Don Chapman and Aaron Heaton went in an entirely different

direction. The aspiring brewery owners decided to specialize in brewing only German beer styles or German-inspired beers. But any thought of their adhering to Germany's strict Reinheitsgebot (beer purity laws) was immediately dismissed. One of their most successful beers is **Snow Drop**, a kottbusser, which is a long-forgotten German style brewed with the addition of honey, oats, and molasses.

The taproom is located just across the parking lot from the brewery, toward the back of a commercial plaza. Grimm Brothers makes the best of the space with an open taproom and beer hall, where barrels are stacked high against the walls not far from a row of dartboards.

The branding aesthetic of Grimm Brothers is an eye-catching one; the brewery paid a skilled artist to create new fairy-tale character for every beer, adding a literary element to branding. In addition to Snow Drop, other year-round beers include **Little Red Cap**, a Düsseldorf altbier; **Fearless Youth**, a bready dunkel; and **The Griffin**, a bright and flavorful traditional Hefeweizen.

LEFT HAND BREWING COMPANY

1265 Boston Ave., Longmont CO 80501; (303) 772-0258; LeftHandBrewing.com
Founded: 1993 **Founders:** Dick Doore and Eric Wallace **Brewers:** Matt Thrall, Jeff Joslin, and Henry Myers **Flagship beers:** IPA, Juicy Goodness, Travelin' Light, Colorful Colorado, Sawtooth Ale, Death Before Disco Porter, Milk Stout, Milk Stout Nitro **Seasonals/special releases:** Peach Beerllini Radler, Oktoberfest Marzen Lager, Good Juju, Wheels Gose 'Round, Fade to Black, Wake Up Dead Imperial Stout, Wake Up Dead Nitro, Chai Milk Stout Nitro **Tours:** Book appointments online or by phone **Taproom hours:** Mon through Sat, 11 a.m. to 9 p.m.; Sun, 11 a.m. to 8 p.m. Bottles and cans to go.

A fun Colorado beer trivia question: What was the original name of Left Hand Brewing? The answer: Indian Peaks. Dick Doore and Eric Wallace, two friends from the Air Force Academy who founded the brewery, started with that name in 1993 in a former meatpacking factory in Longmont. It didn't last long—another brewery used the name for one of its beers. Eventually, the pair settled on Left Hand Brewing Company after Chief Niwot, whose tribe spent winters in the Boulder Valley area. (Niwot is the Arapahoe word for "left handed.") The company opened under its new name in January 1994, but its logo didn't come to reality until 1995 when the company realized its original

artwork wouldn't fit on a bottle cap. Now the red hand is one of the most recognized symbols in the craft beer industry.

Doore, who started with a homebrew kit he received for Christmas in 1990, won a handful of awards in the early years and first brewed a sweet milk stout in 1999. The beer became the inspiration in 2011 for one of the biggest

Beer Lover's Pick

FADE TO BLACK, VOL. 1

Style: Foreign Export Stout
ABV: 8.5 percent
Availability: September through January in cans and on draft

A trip to Left Hand Brewing Company isn't complete without enjoying a Milk Stout Nitro. But the second beer to try if you visit in the colder months is Fade to Black, Vol. 1. The flavors of licorice, molasses, and dark roast finish bone-dry with a moderate hop bite. It's far better than the Guinness typically asso-ciated with the style category and will make you appreciate the complexity in the simple things in life.

Left Hand Brewing Company

innovations in craft beer history: the nitro bottle and, in 2017, the nitro can. The beer's popularity nationwide is hard to underestimate. If a bar has a nitro tap, there's a real good chance it's Left Hand **Milk Stout Nitro**. Whether on tap or in a bottle or can, the tiny bubbles of nitrogen gas that cascade from the bottle to the top give the beer an impenetrable head and creamy mouthfeel. Other styles have expanded into the format, such as **Flamingo Dreams**, a blonde ale.

Now past its 25th anniversary, Left Hand is best known for its dark beers, but the lineup covers a broad cross section and offer flavors for everyone, whether it's the hazy golden ale **Juicy Goodness** or the summer favorite **Travelin' Light** Kölsch-style ale. The taproom is the place to visit for the latest test batches and barrel-aged offerings you can't find in bottles.

LIQUID MECHANICS BREWING COMPANY

297 US 287, Suite 100, Lafayette, CO 80026; (720) 550-7813; LiquidMechanicsBrewing.com
Founded: 2014 **Founders:** David Helden, Eric Briggs, and Seth Townsend **Brewer:** Seth Townsend **Flagship beers:** Amber Altbier, IPA, Hopacity, Hop Nectar, Kölsch **Seasonals/special releases:** Imperial Porter, Peanut Butter Porter, Belgian Double IPA, Gose, Märzen, Fresh Hopped Imperial Red Ale, Sojourn Saison, South German Pils, Barrel Aged Awesomeness, Fresh Hop Imperial Porter, Dark Lager **Tours:** None **Taproom hours:** Mon through Thurs, 2 to 10 p.m.; Fri, 2 to 11 p.m.; Sat, noon to 11 p.m.; Sun, noon to 9 p.m. Growlers, crowlers, cans, and bottles to go.

The three founders of Liquid Mechanics left their day jobs in the biotech and pharmaceutical industries to pursue a professional brewery. Seth Townsend, the brewer, made beer at home for 18 years and won plenty of awards. Now as a professional, he counts more than three dozen medals to his name in a range of styles.

Liquid Mechanics is one of the breweries that's transforming Lafayette into a mini beer hub. Located in a shopping center on a main highway, the brewery pours beer from 14 taps in an open taproom with a great U-shaped bar over which an installation of wood pallets hang, casting interesting shadows on the walls. The garage doors open up to a patio in the warm months, and the place fills with regulars and the sound of live music. It became so popular that the owners needed to expand a couple years after opening.

The beer list keeps rotating with new brews and mainstays. The **Peanut Butter Porter** is one of the bestsellers, a sweet, thick beer that tastes like its name. Another one is **Hop Nectar**, a hazy IPA with more bite than most in the style. The **Kölsch** is a true-to-style beer that is the brewer's go-to option.

ODD13 BREWING

301 E. Simpson St., Lafayette, CO 80026; (303) 997-4164; Odd13Brewing.com
Founded: 2013 **Founders:** Kristin and Ryan Scott **Brewer:** Ryan Scott **Flagship beers:** Codename: Superfan, Intergalactic Juice Hunter, Noob, Vincent Van Couch **Seasonals/special releases:** Eric's Ex-Wife, Hop Troll, Humulus Kalecumber, Codename: Holidayfan, Robot Librarian, QDH Codename: Superfan **Tours:** None **Taproom hours:** Mon, 3 to 9 p.m.; Tues through Thurs, 3 to 10 p.m.; Fri, 1 to 11 p.m.; Sat, noon to 11 p.m.; Sun, noon to 9 p.m. Cans to go.

Odd13 Brewing built its reputation on staying ahead of the curve. It is the first in Colorado to put sour beer in cans. And it claims the mantle as the first in the state to make New England–style IPAs. The haze craze is what helped make Odd13 a beer destination in Colorado. **Codename: Superfan** is its bestseller, accounting for as much as 40 percent of its beer sales at one point. Brewer and owner Ryan Scott continually likes to play with hops, making different iterations of Superfan or entirely different hazy IPAs, altering the yeast and hops to make beers such as **Intergalactic Juice Hunter**, a double with lactose added to add an even more soft and round mouthfeel.

The push to make something new keeps the 16 taps constantly rotating at Odd13's tasting room in Lafayette. A new rotating beer appears every month, whether an IPA or a sour, often with fruit added, and each year, only about half the beers continue to make an appearance. Scott brewed on a converted

Beer Lover's Pick

CODENAME: SUPERFAN

Style: Hazy IPA

ABV: 6.5 percent

Availability: Year-round on draft and in cans

Codename: Superfan offers the best of both hazy IPA worlds. It's soft but still with a present bitterness. It's a full mouthfeel, but it's not too thick. It's big in fruit aroma and flavor but not sweet. Overall, it's a New England–style IPA that you can drink more than one at a time, which isn't always true at

other breweries. The hops are primarily citra and simcoe with a dose of papaya and dankness from eukanot.

dairy system but is building out much larger capacity with larger fermenters to help meet demand. Even though hop experimentation dominates, the menu includes mixed-culture-fermentation sours, saisons, stouts, lagers, and even barrel-aged beers. The artwork on the logo is as fun to look at as the beer, some of which is drawn by Kyrie Wozab, an Odd13 beertender and artist.

OSKAR BLUES BREWERY

1800 Pike Rd., #B, Longmont, CO 80501; (303) 776-1914; OskarBlues.com
Taproom hours: Mon through Fri, 10 a.m. to 8 p.m.; Sat and Sun, noon to 8 p.m. Crowlers and cans to go.
921 Pearl St. Boulder, CO 80302; (720) 645-1749
Taproom hours: Sun through Thurs, 11 a.m. to 11 p.m.; Fri and Sat, 11 a.m. to midnight. Crowlers and cans to go.
Founded: 1997 **Founder:** Dale Katechis **Brewer:** Tim Matthews
Flagship beers: Dale's Pale Ale, Old Chub, Mama's Little Yella Pils, Pinner, G'Knight **Seasonals/special releases:** Ten Fidy, Barrel-Aged Ten Fidy, Fugli, Death By Coconut, Hotbox Coffee Porter **Tours (Longmont location):** Mon through Fri, 4 p.m.; Sat and Sun, 2 p.m., 3 p.m., 4 p.m., and 5 p.m.

Oskar Blues is synonymous with being the first craft brewery to put its beer in cans. The brewery blazed the trail at a time when most in the craft beer community thought cans were appropriate only for cheap, light lagers. Oskar Blues put a well-hopped beer, **Dale's Pale Ale**, in the can. With the bold move, Oskar Blues owner and founder Dale Katechis elevated his small

brewery in Lyons to national interest. That was 2002. Now Oskar Blues is one of the dominant breweries in America, owner of three brew houses (including Brevard, North Carolina, and Austin, Texas) as well as the ringleader of a collective of craft breweries across the country known as Canarchy.

The origin story starts in Lyons, where Katechis opened a Cajun restaurant in 1997 and asked Left Hand Brewing to make the house beer. Two years later, he partnered with a homebrewer to start his own operation and eventually moved the brewery to Longmont. **Old Chub**, a full-bodied, malty, and somewhat smoky Scotch ale, followed. The imperial red IPA **G'Knight** (named for famed Colorado brewer Gordon Knight) is making a comeback as a malty, dry-hopped, and balanced beer. And **Pinner** is one of the premier examples of a session IPA with a light body and big, bright hop character. Keeping with the times, Oskar Blues makes a number of small-batch variants that draw hordes on release day, such as **Rum-Barrel Aged Death By Coconut** and **Barrel-Aged Mocha Ten Fidy**.

The cans—including its new 32-ounce crowlers (a riff on growlers)—fit the brewery's affinity for the active lifestyle, like Katechis's favorite, mountain biking. And it actually is a perfect vessel for beer, keeping out light and oxygen,

Beer Lover's Pick

PINNER THROWBACK IPA

Style: Session IPA
ABV: 4.9 percent
Availability: Year-round in cans and on draft

The oft-repeated knock on craft beer is that it's not sessionable or drinkable for longer periods of time, because it's too full-bodied, too full-flavored, or too boozy. In those situations, most people move to lagers. But Pinner is the answer for those who want to drink IPAs all day  long. And not watered-down session versions but one that packs more flavor than some full-throttled IPAs. The citrus and peppery hop flavors are complemented by a soft bread malt in a crushable format at less than 5 percent ABV.

Oskar Blues Brewery

allowing it to stay fresh longer. But Oskar Blues is known by much more than its cans now. The company has spin-off spirits and soda lines as well as coffee roasters, burger bars, and numerous other restaurant operations, including a few in the Denver area. A second taproom is open in downtown Boulder.

VERBOTEN BREWING & BARREL PROJECT

125 E. 5th St., Loveland, CO 80537; (970) 775-7371; VerbotenBrewing.com
Founded: 2013 **Founders:** Angie and Josh Grenz and Jason Bowser
Brewer: Josh Grenz **Flagship beers:** Killer Boots, Brew #2, You Can't Handle the Kölsch, Thinking of Something Orange, Two Fives, Stealth Haze **Seasonal/special releases:** Angry Banjo, Fruit for the People, In Love with Summer, Anybody Want a Peanut?, Somebody to Love, A Belgian to Love, Run by Fruiting series, Roll in Ze' Hay, Pure Imagination, Little Nonsense **Tours:** Fri through Sun, 3 p.m., 4 p.m., and 5 p.m. **Taproom hours:** Sun and Mon, noon to 9 p.m.; Tues through Thurs, noon to 10 p.m.; Fri and Sat, 11 a.m. to 11 p.m. Growlers and bottles to go.

B eer for all" is the mantra at Verboten Brewing & Barrel Project in Loveland. The brewery's motto speaks to the approachability of the beers on the menu and its seasonality. A small core lineup of standard offerings gives way to 10 or so special beers on tap with seasonal ingredients, such as the house gose **Roll in Ze' Hay** with watermelons or blueberries.

Despite the desire for mass appeal, the brewery's name actually speaks to its desire to draw outside the lines. Verboten refers to the forbidden ingredients from the days of the German beer purity laws, and the brewery makes a point to use them—whether fruit, spice, or more—in its brews. One of the brewery's most distinct beers is Angry Banjo, a hybrid Kentucky Common, which is one of the few native beers styles to America. The beer is made with American malts and flaked rye (instead of the style's traditional corn) as well as chocolate and caramel malts to make a darker riff on a cream ale.

The brewery started small on a three-barrel system but graduated to a larger operation in a new downtown Loveland location that gives it room to produce packaged beers, most of which are in 22-ounce bombers.

WELDWERKS BREWING COMPANY

508 8th Ave., Greeley, CO 80631; (970) 460-6345
3043 W. Pikes Peak Ave., Colorado Springs, CO 80904;
WeldWerksBrewing.com
Founded: 2015 **Founders:** Neil Fisher and Colin Jones **Brewers:** Neil Fisher and Arne Garlick **Flagship beers:** Juicy Bits and Hefeweizen **Seasonals/special releases:** Achromatic series, Medianoche series, DDH Juicy Bits, Extra Extra Juicy Bits, Steambarrel, Fruited Berliner series, Gose series **Tours:** Saturdays **Taproom:** Mon through Thurs, noon to 9 p.m.; Fri and Sat, noon to 10 p.m.; Sun, noon to 7 p.m. Bottles and cans to go.

WeldWerks Brewing is considered one of the best—if not the best—breweries in Colorado. The reasons are simple. First, WeldWerks makes great beer. The brewery is best known for hazy IPAs and decadent stouts, but it also excels in traditional styles. Second, it's willing to push the boundaries. From milkshake IPAs and huge dry-hopped beers to fruited Berliner weisses and barrel-aged adjunct stouts, the styles and flavors are innovative and interesting. Third, it makes a large number of beers that keeps the menu evolving. In 2018, the brewery set a goal to make 100 different beers—only to top that number in nine months. And finally, WeldWerks cultivates a community in rural Greeley with a welcoming taproom and great service.

It's not easy to put all these ingredients together, but founders Neil Fisher and Colin Jones managed to make it happen and build a brewery that now boasts a national fan base. The brewery offers regular 16-ounce can releases and hosts a number of special events, the latter attracting long lines of beer fans from Colorado and neighboring states.

The first beer to try is **Juicy Bits**, a New England–style IPA that is loaded with citrus hop flavors and aroma and soft, not bitter, in mouthfeel. The turbid appearance also fits its name. The brewery makes many variations of its flagship that allows for an exploration of hop varieties. If you prefer

Beer Lover's Pick

JUICY BITS

Style: New England–Style IPA
ABV: 6.5 percent
Availability: Year-round on draft and often in cans

The name of this beer tells the story. It's loaded with so many hops and a pillowy soft mouthfeel that it's practically juice. Where other hazy IPAs can still finish with a bite, this one is all mellow with just a touch of bitterness. The base beer is the flagship, but the variations—whether Extra Extra Juicy Bits or Quadruple Dry-Hopped Juicy Bits—will only continue to amaze as a showcase of the style.

traditional beers, the **Puesta del Sol** is a Vienna lager for any occasion, and the **Hefeweizen** is a great example of the modern style. The brewery makes two different stout series that you can't miss: **Achromatic** features adjuncts like peanut butter and spices, and **Medianoche** is the decadent and complex barrel-aged series.

WeldWerks announced in early 2019 that it would open a satellite taproom in Colorado Springs. It won't brew at the location but will pour its popular beer.

WILEY ROOTS BREWING COMPANY

625 3rd St., Unit D, Greeley, CO 80631; (970) 515-7315; WileyRoots.com
Founded: 2013 **Founders:** Kyle and Miranda Carbaugh **Brewer:** Kyle Carbaugh **Flagship beers:** Super 77, Funk Yo Couch **Seasonals/special releases:** Pseudonym, Packed with Peaches, Cinnamonsta, Slush series, High Fidelity DIPA, Pyromonstah, Rapid Transit, Burnet Down, DDH 1320, Trygonometry, Mail Order Mule **Tours:** None **Taproom:** Wed and Thurs, 4 to 10 p.m.; Fri and Sat, noon to 11 p.m.; Sun, 1 to 8 p.m. Bottles and cans to go.

Wiley Roots is located a short walk from WeldWerks Brewing to the other side of the train tracks in an old industrial part of Greeley. It makes for a great one-two punch in a small, rural town where you wouldn't

typically go looking for great beer. Wiley Roots started small but built larger to make room for a huge lineup with hop-crazed hazy IPAs, decadent dessert stouts, and bright, sour beers—many of them available for purchase at the brewery.

But even at the start, Wiley Roots made an early mark with a medal in its first year and three more in next five years. The classic American wheat ale called **Super 77** garnered initial attention, but now it's the brewery's experimental beers—including its **Funk Yo Couch** series of mixed-culture Brett sours—that draw honors and crowds.

In the warm months, the taproom doors open to a beer garden of sorts along the train tracks. The menu behind the bar is loaded with different options, from the wheat and hazy double IPA to a sour with limes and ginger and a barrel-aged imperial stout. On the dark end of the beer spectrum, **Cinnamonsta** is a crowd favorite, an imperial stout with cinnamon that is a great pop of sweet and spice. The variants on popular styles, as well as the collaborations, keep a weekday crowd of regulars and a weekend crowd of brew tourists quite happy.

dark chocolate–covered Brazil-nut flavors that permeate the beer. The **Blood Orange IPA** is another favorite with five different hops, as well as blood orange peels.

A popular Colorado winter release, **Cocoa Porter**, is a low-bitterness American porter, brewed with a healthy amount of cocoa. The resulting dark-brown pour is a smooth drink, laden with milk chocolate and mocha aroma and flavor. This 5.7 percent ABV beer is a must-try for chocolate beer lovers.

WESTBOUND & DOWN BREWING COMPANY

1617 Miner St., Idaho Springs, CO 80452; (720) 502-3121; WestboundAndDown.com
956 Santa Fe Dr., Denver, CO 80204
Founded: 2015 **Founders:** Geoff McFarlane, Dan Brown, and Jed MacArthur **Brewer:** Jake Gardner **Flagship beers:** Colorado Pale Ale, Double IPA, Porter, Another IPA, Don't Hassle the Hef, Bel-Hop Pop Belgian Strong, Belgian Pale **Seasonals/special releases:** Solera Saison, Framboat Drinks, Soberish Monk, General MacArthur's Scotch Ale, The Angry Dan Brown Ale, Fruited Berliner Weisse, Vers L'Ouest Tripel, Den'var Pils **Tours:** None **Taproom hours:** Mon through Sun, 11 a.m. to 10 p.m. Growlers and crowlers to go.

A step from the quaint downtown of the old mining town of Idaho Springs and inside the door at Westbound & Down Brewing is like a time portal from past to present. The brewery's sleek look and clean lines, with brick walls painted white, modern lighting, and wood and metal high-top tables, are a departure from the dusty town. The back features two large garage doors that open in the summer to showcase shiny brewing tanks. It sounds like it belongs in the big city—and Westbound & Down is expanding to a second Denver location on Santa Fe Drive.

The Idaho Springs location manages to retain a bit of its grit thanks to a partnership with the historic Buffalo Restaurant & Bar, which underwent a renovation to make it more modern. The two watering holes are connected in the middle, and the latter provides the kitchen for both. The food menu is a blend, too. The items—think green chili cheese fries, buffalo chicken nachos, burgers, and fried chicken—are an upscale feel in execution and presentation on traditional bar fare.

The beer is increasingly taking an elevated approach with barrel-aged offerings, fruited Berliner weisse beers, and a growing emphasis on sours, thanks in part to a collaboration with Amalgam, a Denver brewery that is only open to the public sporadically. But the menu covers the range of styles, and the **Colorado Pale Ale**, a house IPA, and other lighter offers remain a go-to pint for travelers.

Westbound & Down is located a couple blocks from Tommyknocker, just down Miner Street, the main thoroughfare through town. The combination allows for a mini brewery tour after hitting the trails or ski resorts along the I-70 mountain corridor—if you have a responsible driver.

THE BARREL

251 Moraine Ave., Estes Park, CO 80517; (970) 616-2090;
TheBarrel.Beer
1710 29th St., Boulder, CO 80301; (720) 563-1812
Taps: 60 **Bottles/cans:** 12

The Barrel is a beer bar located in a shipping container—actually, two different shipping containers, one in Estes Park and one in Boulder. The one to make sure to visit is Estes Park, just outside Rocky Mountain National Park. It's located on Moraine Avenue, just a block or so up the hill from the main downtown intersection and, from the opposite direction, just around the corner from a couple of local breweries. In other words, it's well positioned for a beer after hiking, driving, or elk watching in the park.

The Barrel started outside with the container as the bar and picnic tables in an open courtyard as the seating—which meant you needed to watch the weather. A sunny day with live music on the weekend is the best. But on a rainy day, the container didn't have many seats under the cover, and if it was really cold, the taps wouldn't pour. Thankfully, The Barrel's expansion into a neighboring building helped alleviate the trouble.

The bar features at least 60 taps and a couple handfuls of bottled or canned beer. The list includes gluten-free, ciders, and meads as well as wine and sodas. The breweries on the list are heavy hitters with big-name brews from the likes of Ommegang, Stone, and Melvin and a solid lineup of Colorado breweries, particularly from the northern Front Range.

OSKAR BLUES HOME MADE LIQUIDS & SOLIDS

**1555 S. Hover Rd., Longmont, CO 80501; (303) 485-9400;
OskarBlues.com
Taps:** 44

Oskar Blues is so much more than a brewery. And that's clear at its hometown Home Made Liquids & Solids restaurant—as well as a host of other locations that constitute its Oskar Blues Fooderies empire.

The family includes a range of enterprises, each with its own appeal. Oskar Blues Grill & Brew is the traditional outfit with locations in Denver, Colorado Springs, and Lyons—which is the original. Chubuger is a burger bar in Longmont and Denver. Cyclhops is a "bike cantina" with tacos, tequila, craft beer, and a bike shop in Longmont. Hotbox Roasters serves coffee, doughnuts, and beer in Denver. The Black Buzzard is a restaurant and bar with a downstairs music venue in Denver. And then there's a taproom and restaurant in downtown Boulder.

The Home Made Liquids & Solids location is one of the best places to visit—just look for a giant silo wrapped in the Oskar Blues logo. It features more than 40 taps, a well-curated list of national and Colorado breweries with a variety of styles to keep your palate interested and a big group satisfied. The southern barbecue–inspired menu is perfectly Oskar Blues, an ode to founder Dale Katechis's Alabama roots. The appetizers include crab cakes with green tomatoes, fried pickles, and wings with a variety of beer-inspired sauces. The main dishes include the standard fare from soups and salads to pizzas and burgers. The whiskey-barrel and applewood-smoked meats are a specialty with ribs, chicken, brisket, and pulled pork as great options. The sides include real dirty rice, collard greens, cheesy mac, fritters, and sweet potato fries.

South Central

Buena Vista, Colorado Springs, Divide, Manitou Springs, Monument, Poncha Springs, Pueblo, and Salida

The southeastern and central regions of Colorado are anchored by two craft beer destinations: Colorado Springs and the central mountains area. The beer scene in Colorado Springs fits a more traditional approach with brewpubs and breweries focusing on approachable beer meant for a wider audience and family experiences. But it's beginning to evolve and feature more edgier brews for those who appreciate innovation. A sample of both are reflected in this section. It is also home to one of the state's better beer makers, TRiNiTY, a sour expert. In the central mountains, a robust craft beer scene is developing in one of the state's adventure hubs. Buena Vista, located between the Arkansas River on the east side and the towering Collegiate Peaks range on the west, is home to a great craft beer bar and a brewery that reflect its western outpost history and outdoor spirit. The brew trail continues south to nearby Salida and Poncha Springs, where a handful of breweries are keeping river guides, tourists, and

MOUNTAIN FOLK WELL HYDRATED. MUCH OF THE BREWING CULTURE ACROSS THIS REGION CONTINUES TO EVOLVE, EVEN IN SMALLER CITIES AND RURAL OUTPOSTS, SUCH AS PUEBLO, WHERE BREWERS ARE ESTABLISHING OPERATIONS THAT MAY MATURE INTO GREAT BEER DESTINATIONS IN THE FUTURE.

BRISTOL BREWING COMPANY

1604 S. Cascade Ave., Colorado Springs, CO 80905; (719) 633-2555; BristolBrewing.com

Founded: 1994 **Founder:** Mike Bristol **Brewers:** Mike Bristol and Jeff Adams **Flagship beers:** Laughing Lab Scottish Ale, Red Rocket Pale Ale, Beehive Honey Wheat, Compass IPA, Ivywild School Tropical Pale Ale **Seasonals/special releases:** Winter Warlock Oatmeal Stout, Yellow Kite Summer Pils, Red Baron Octoberfest Lager, Belgian series, Forgotten Genius series, Christmas Ale, Old No. 23 Barleywine **Tours:** None **Taproom hours:** Sun through Thurs, 11 a.m. to 10 p.m.; Fri and Sat, 11 a.m. to 11 p.m. Growlers, cans, and bottles to go.

Bristol was founded in 1994 by Mike Bristol, another refugee of the corporate world who decided that opening a brewery was more his speed. Located in Colorado Springs, Bristol and his namesake brewery are known for three things: It's family-owned, independent and only available in Colorado. The community focus is obvious in its charity beer series. And it's located in the Ivywild School, a sand-colored brick elementary school built in 1916 that's now a community marketplace and gathering spot. The Bristol Pub at the north end of the building proudly serves beer in former classrooms and

LAUGHING LAB SCOTTISH ALE

Style: Scottish Ale

ABV: 5.4 percent

Availability: Available year-round on tap and in bottles

Laughing Lab is a rust-colored, Scottish-style ale that is sweet but not too overpowering. The flavors are rich with sweet fudge, hazelnut, biscuit, and caramel notes as well as a smooth, velvety finish. The description skews toward moments in front of a campfire or when the air gets a chill, but it's surprisingly drinkable year-round. The beer won nine GABF medals since 1994 and acts as the antithesis to overhopped beers, showcasing the joy of malt flavors.

features an outdoor patio. The brewery doubled its size when it moved into the new location in 2013 and now is a ubiquitous Colorado beer name with wide distribution within the state's borders.

Laughing Lab Scottish Ale is one of the most awarded beers in the nation and is the first pour to order when you visit. The standard styles on the board are balanced by a range of rotating series that keep the flavors fresh. A newer mainstay is the **Ivywild School Tropical Pale Ale**, which draws tangerine and grapefruit flavors from mandarina bavaria, citra, mosaic, and azacca hops without being too bitter. The brewery also serves food—in a menu that starts with a composition notebook–style design no less.

ELEVATION BEER COMPANY

115 Pahlone Pkwy., Poncha Springs, CO 81242; (719) 539-5258; ElevationBeerCo.com

Founded: 2012 **Founders:** Xandy and Sheila Bustamante, Carlin Walsh, and Christian Koch **Brewer:** Christian Koch **Flagship beers:** Elevation Pilsner, 8 Second Kölsch, Wave Wheel Wit, First Cast, Little Mo' **Seasonals/special releases:** Double IPA, Apis IV, Señorita, Raspberry Gulch, False Summit, Oil Man, Signal de Botrange, Acide, Red Wine Barrel Aged Apis IV **Tours:** By appointment **Taproom hours:** Mon through Sun, noon to 8 p.m.

E levation Beer is a true mountain brewery. When it opened, its beers were organized by ski slope ratings. The moderate-difficulty blue square signifies regular beers, and the double black diamonds represent special challenging brews. The designs are still evident, even if the system is now less official, and the brewery is the official beer maker for the local ski resort, Monarch Mountain. Others beers were named for outdoor pursuits, whether fishing or kayaking. It's fitting given that the region where the brewery is located is one of the top destinations in the state for these pursuits.

Beer Lover's Pick

8 SECOND KÖLSCH

Style: Kölsch-Style Ale
ABV: 5 percent
Availability: Year-round on draft and in cans

Elevation's head brewer, Christian Koch, initially came to love Kölsch during his travels in Cologne, Germany, where the style calls home. The beer is a hybrid—an ale fermented warm but then conditioned cold like a lager. The result is a light-colored beer with a touch of hop character and a crisp finish. It's a delicate style that's hard to execute but one you can return to time after time.

The styles are ideal for those who like to play because they are sold in cans. **8 Second Kölsch** and **Wave Wheel Wit** are go-to beers for the river when you want something cold that won't make you slip on the rocks. And **Little Mo'** is a roast-flavored porter that drinks easy for the style. But it's the more nuanced beers that make Elevation rise above other local breweries. **False Summit** is a quadrupel Belgian ale aged in bourbon barrels with rich caramel, vanilla candy, and oak tannins, while **Oil Man** is an imperial stout aged in bourbon barrels that pours like the namesake liquid with a rich brown head of foam.

The brewery is situated not far from a crossroads to outdoor adventures outside Salida and pours from 16 taps. But it also sells beer to go—which is good because sitting inside a brewery in this outdoor hub is difficult to do.

GOAT PATCH BREWING COMPANY

2727 N. Cascade Ave., #123, Colorado Springs, CO 80907; (719) 471-4628; GoatPatchBrewing.com
Founded: 2016 **Founders:** Justin and Jen Grant, Darren and Cate Baze, and Pete King **Brewers:** Darren Baze and Dylan Houghton **Flagship beers:** Blonde Ale, It Takes a Tribe Red Ale **Seasonals/ special releases:** Belgian Wit, Honeybush Belgian Summer Ale, Smoked ESB, Stout, Mocha Latte Stout, Goat Patch IPA, Blood Orange IPA, Double IPA **Tours:** None **Taproom hours:** Mon through Thurs, noon to 9 p.m.; Fri, noon to 11 p.m.; Sat, 11 a.m. to 11 p.m.; Sun, 11 a.m. to 8 p.m. Growlers and crowlers to go.

Darren Baze better not shave. His three-foot-long "goat patch"–style beard is the namesake for this Colorado Springs brewery and well-known in town. If you see him, be sure to ask him how long he's been growing it. Before joining Goat Patch Brewing, he spent 13 years in the industry, including stints at three local breweries: Bristol, Trinity, and Colorado Mountain. His new place specializes in balanced brews, like the award-winning flagship red ale known as **It Takes a Tribe**.

Goat Patch is one of the new kids on the block on the Colorado Springs beer scene, located in the auditorium of the old Lincoln Elementary School north of downtown. The taproom is simple and elegant with seats at a dark-wood bar and other tables. When it's warm, the brewery opens large garage doors onto a patio on the parking lot side. From the start, it focused on the community. And each Tuesday, it runs a promotion called "Bleating Heart" night, in which a portion of pint sales go toward local nonprofits and other efforts to support area organizations.

As a newcomer, the beer list is still evolving, but it offers a mix of popular new styles, like fruited and hazy IPAs, as well as more traditional beers. Baze, the brewer, has experience with everything from big-hopped IPAs to sours, so look for more diversity and interesting beers to come.

PARADOX BEER COMPANY

10 Buffalo Ct., Divide, CO 80814; (719) 686-8081; ParadoxBeerCompany.com
Founded: 2012 **Founders:** Jeff Aragon, Brian Horton, and David Hudson **Brewers:** Jeff Aragon and Brian Horton **Flagship beers:** None **Seasonals/special releases:** Skully series, Future Knowledge series, La Fiesta, Fistful of Juice, Dunk Your Face **Tours:** None **Taproom hours:** Sun and Mon, 11 a.m. to 9 p.m.; Thurs, 11 a.m. to 9 p.m.; Fri and Sat, 11 a.m. to 10 p.m. Bottles to go.

From its three-acre estate on a hill overlooking the vast valley in Divide and with Pikes Peak in the distance, Paradox Beer specializes in unique sour and farmhouse beers that are barrel-aged and bottle-conditioned.

Put more simply, it's making old styles new again, hence the name. The brewery embraces traditional brewing techniques, using wild and spontaneous fermentation and focusing on barrel aging. It's funky beer located in the middle of the mountains. And for beer fans who want to try something new each time, this is the place to go. Paradox doesn't often brew the same beer twice and numbers its main **Skully** series so you don't miss one.

The brewery's expansion to this new location in 2015 allowed it to add massive oak foeders to age beer as well as 200-plus oak barrels and a custom-built spontaneous fermentation coolship to make beers punctuated with the natural terroir at 9,000 feet. The brewery offers a handful of clean beers, whether lagers or IPAs, but the special focus is the bottled beers with sours that have featured pomegranate juice and tangerine peels or passion fruit and wine-barrel aging. The one-off nature of the beer means some hit the mark and others get close, but the experimentation keeps it interesting.

The brewery posts more limited hours in the winter, but the summer months are the time to visit. The brewery opens into a courtyard with picnic tables and umbrellas, yard games, and chairs made from barrels that sit in front of a massive stone fireplace. A limited food menu also is available.

BRUES ALEHOUSE BREWING COMPANY

120 Riverwalk Place, Pueblo, CO 81003; (719) 924-9670; BruesAleHouse.com
Founded: 2015 **Founders:** Tony and Marty Garcia **Brewer:** Tony Garcia **Flagship beers:** Prohibition Lager, Valve-3 Amber Ale, Boneman Tripel, Leadhead IPA, Nitro Manthers **Seasonals/special releases:** Pat Down Pale Ale, Manthers Stout, Storyteller Stout, Coconut Vanilla Storyteller Stout, Mexican Chocolate Storyteller Stout, Pinehopple Express, Oude Ruby Cherry Ale **Tours:** None **Taproom hours:** Sun through Thurs, 8 a.m. to 10 p.m.; Fri and Sat, 8 a.m. to midnight. Growlers and crowlers to go.

Brues Alehouse is an oasis in a place where light beer sold in 30-packs still dominates. In southern Colorado, Pueblo is the largest city, but its beer scene is still behind the times. Outside Shamrock Brewing, the longtime Irish pub and brewery, the city doesn't have many other options.

Brues Alehouse is located in the Riverwalk district, a development that is revitalizing this old steel town, and occupies the city's old police building and jail. The brewpub offers food, music, and beer. It actually opens first thing for breakfast with a bakery and coffee shop. The rooftop patio is the place to be when the sun sets and it begins to cool down.

The beer and food is seen as one in the same with an inventive approach to both. The beer menu offers the basics and a few fun options, including a handful of barrel-aged beers. The **Leadhead IPA** presents a surprisingly lively and quenching bite. The **Storyteller Stout** is best in the barrel-aged options, whether the coconut or the Mexican chocolate options. The house brews are accentuated with a handful of rotating guest taps of craft beers. And you'd be remiss not to order a beer cocktail, such as Citrus Smash, which starts with the **Boneman Tripel** and gets interesting with Leopold Peach Whiskey, orange, lemon, lime, mint, and simple syrup.

CERBERUS BREWING COMPANY

702 W. Colorado Ave., Colorado Springs, CO 80905; (719) 636-2337; CerberusBrewingCo.com
Founded: 2016 **Founders:** Tom Halfast, Josh Adamski, Cindy Geiser, and Jerry Morris **Brewers:** Josh Adamski and Taylor Donner **Flagship beers:** No Big Deal Kölsch, Tiny Umbrella Party IPA, Elysium IPA **Seasonals/special releases:** Perpetual Cycle Pils, Ginger Beer, Demeter, Hoka Hey IPA, Hel Imperial Stout, Double Dog, Reminiscent Cream Ale **Tours:** None **Taproom hours:** Sun through Thurs, 11 a.m. to 10 p.m.; Fri and Sat, 11 a.m. to 11 p.m. Crowlers to go.

It just seems appropriate that Cerberus Brewing, named for the mythical three-headed dog, is located in a former veterinarian hospital. The few repurposed cages are one of the only details that remain at the brewpub after a remodel, though. The space inside is tight with a compact brewing lab, small dining area, and eight-seat bar that glows with red lights. But the highlight is the mulched outdoor play yard, often full of dogs, where wooden Adirondack chairs and picnic tables are arranged underneath umbrellas.

The brewpub pours 24 taps at the bar, along with liquor and wine. The brews cover a range of styles with a recent menu featuring cream ale, kölsch, gose, saison, California common, hazy IPA, and stout. A handful of guest taps from well-known Colorado breweries help fill the gaps. The early reviews are good, and brewer Josh Adamski continues to refine its recipes and offerings, always with an eye to something new. He previously served as the manager at Brewer's Republic, a popular craft beer bar in town, and is a longtime homebrewer.

The food is good with casual fare like beer pretzels with cheddar ale and mustard dipping sauces and IPA bacon bites. The heart of the menu is burgers and sandwiches, such as Colorado lamb sliders, but includes nice plates of local trout, steak, and gnocchi.

EDDYLINE RESTAURANT & BREWERY

102 Linderman Ave., Buena Vista, CO 81211; (719) 966-6018;
EddylineBrewing.com
926 S. Main St., Buena Vista, CO 81211; (719) 966-6000;
EddylineRestaurant.com
Founded: 2009 **Founders:** Mic and Molley Heynekamp **Brewer:** Brian
England **Flagship beers:** Crank Yanker IPA, Epic Day Double IPA, River
Runners Pale Ale, Grapefruit Yanker IPA, Raspberry Wheat **Seasonals/
special releases:** Boater Beer Pilsner, Jolly Roger Black Lager, Kickin'
Back Amber Lager, Pumpkin Patch Ale, 14'er Java Stout **Tours:** On
request **Taproom hours:** Mon through Sun, 11 a.m. to 9 p.m. Cans and
growlers to go.

Eddyline Restaurant & Brewery is located in the outdoor nexus of Buena
Vista. And it embraces the lifestyle in its beers. The brewery is a decade old
now and fills two locations. The restaurant is located on South Main Street, a
new development along the Arkansas River with a park, shops, and a boutique
hotel. And the brewery is located to the west on the other side of US 24, the
north-to-south thoroughfare through town.

The two locations reflect Eddyline's significant growth from a three-barrel
brewing system to multiple major expansions that now give it the capacity to
expand to 40,000 barrels. The extra room gave the brewery the ability to can
its showcase IPA, **Crank Yanker**, a bold, 7.8 percent ABV, high-IBU American

style. It strikes a pleasing balance with a residual malt sweetness and layered pine-evoking, hop-derived bite and aroma.

The restaurant offers up pecan wood–fired pizzas as well as salads and pub snacks like nachos, spiced tots and green chili artichoke dip to pair with the beer. And in the summer, the brewery's beer garden features an outdoor bar, seating area, and stage that often has live music.

MANITOU BREWING COMPANY

725 Manitou Ave., Manitou Springs, CO 80829; (719) 282-7709; Manitou-Brewing.com
Founded: 2014 **Founder:** Dominic Koh **Brewer:** Dominic Koh
Flagship beers: High Ground IPA, Burro Barn Brown Ale, Saison, Little Wit Crazy, A-Frame Amber Ale, Barr Trail Pale Ale **Seasonals/special releases:** Summer Honey Wheat, Captain Harrill's Baltic Porter, Cerise Mousseux Nouveau, Biere de Garde **Tours:** None **Taproom hours:** Mon through Thurs, noon to 9 p.m.; Fri, noon to 11 p.m.; Sat, 11 a.m. to 11 p.m.; Sun, 11 a.m. to 9 p.m. Growlers to go.

Manitou Brewing sits at the foot of Pikes Peak, a 14,115-foot behemoth that looms over Colorado Springs and central Colorado and even is visible from Denver on a clear day. The brewery is located in Manitou Springs, a quaint gateway town for the half million visitors each year who ascend what is known as America's most famous mountain, whether by car or cog railway. And it's not far from the popular Manitou Incline, a 2,744-step climb that gains 2,000 feet in elevation in less than a mile.

Whether you're summiting the mountain or climbing the incline, you'll earn a beer inside the cozy taproom or out on the shaded patio at Manitou Brewing once you're down. The brewpub manages to produce beers bigger and better than its small size with the help of a foeder and barrel-aging program that keeps the tap list diverse. It's situated in the former Manitou Burro Line from the late 1800s where visitors could rent a burro and ride to the top of Pikes Peak. The **Burro Barn Brown Ale** is named in the location's honor and delivers a full-bodied ale with rich roasted toffee flavors. The **High Ground IPA** is one of the best beers to get. It delivers a huge hop flavor and gets a loaded dry hop to boost the aroma. The menu offers a number of hearty items to replace the calories you lost climbing, whether the specialty fries, Pikes Peak chicken sandwich, or pulled pork tacos.

PHANTOM CANYON BREWING COMPANY

2 E. Pikes Peak Ave., Colorado Springs, CO 80903; (719)
635-2800; PhantomCanyon.com
Founded: 1993 **Founders:** Mark Schiffler and John Hickenlooper
Brewers: Alan Stiles, Troy Johnson, and Ryan Emley **Flagship beers:**
Dos Lunas, Alpenglow, Box Car, Streamliner IPA **Seasonals/special
releases:** Foozoo, Continuum White Ale, Chucks Wiser, Czech Yo Self,
Squirty McGee, Noriega, Ring of Fire, Roadmaster, Boxcar, Ol Red Beard,
Pump It Up, Wookie Milk, Ewan McTeagle's, Silo J, Cyborg Sea Dog,
After Midnight, Johnson's Farm, Caveman Saga **Tours:** By appointment
Taproom hours: Sun through Thurs, 11 a.m. to 10 p.m.; Fri and Sat,
11 a.m. to 11 p.m. Growlers to go.

When you enter the corner street doors of Phantom Canyon Brewing Company, positioned proudly in the heart of downtown Colorado Springs, it's hard to imagine that the historic building was once hours away from demolition. Its future as one of the first brewpubs in Colorado was thankfully secured in large part by John Hickenlooper, the founder of Wynkoop Brewing Company in Denver, who went on to become the mayor and governor. Hickenlooper bought the Cheyenne Building, and in 1993, Phantom Canyon opened for business.

Phantom Canyon celebrates its status as the city's original brewpub, and it helped inspire a new generation of restaurant owners to begin utilizing

Beer Lover's Pick

JOHNSON'S FARM
Style: Kettle Sour
ABV: 6.9 percent
Availability: Limited

Don't knock pink beer. Johnson's Farm is a sour with so many raspberries—480 pounds to be exact—that it turned pink. The beer is produced from a sour mash and kettle soured to make it tart and refreshing with a strong berry flavor. It's a great beer for the warm months—or any month if you are a sour fanatic.

the long-ignored buildings in the area. The brewery features a small sidewalk seating area at street level and an open-air balcony on the second floor.

Phantom Canyon offers 14 or more beers on tap at any given time, including four year-round beers: **Dos Lunas**, a Mexican lager; **Alpenglow**, a hefeweizen; **Box Car**, an English special bitter; and the **Streamliner IPA**. All the recipes have been honed over many years and represent solid renditions of their respective styles. For the true geek adventurer, though, it's the ever-changing and exciting selection of special beers that pour at Phantom Canyon that will hold the most appeal. Two examples: a barrel-aged imperial ginger wheat called **Cyborg Sea Dog** and a Brett sour named **Caveman Saga**. The brewpub serves brunch, lunch, and dinner with a standard menu that offers something for everyone.

PIKES PEAK BREWING CO.

1756 Lake Woodmoor Dr., Monument, CO 80132; (719) 208-4098; PikesPeakBrewing.com
Founded: 2011 **Founder:** Chris Wright **Brewers:** Chris Wright and Alan Windhausen **Flagship beers:** Elephant Rock, Devils Head Red Ale, Gold Rush, Summit House Oatmeal Stout, Ascent Pale Ale, 38 Faces IPA **Seasonals/special releases:** Coffee Porter, Paddo O The Peak, Meadowgrass Jam Session IPA, Highlander Scottish, Rocky Wheat, Bear Creek Porter, Local 5 Pale Ale, America The Pale (And Beautiful), Oktoberfest, Kissing Camels, Adaman Ale, Hot Shot Green Chili Beer, Tava, Old Stage Stout **Tours:** On request **Taproom hours:** Mon through Thurs, 11 a.m. to 9 p.m.; Fri and Sat, 11 a.m. to 11 p.m.; Sun, noon to 9 p.m. Cans, crowlers, and growlers to go.

Pikes Peak Brewing Co. is located 20 miles north of Colorado Springs along I-25, making it an easy stop for those traveling south from Denver. Founder and brewer Chris Wright wanted the brewery taproom to evoke the comfortable and welcoming vibe of a cozy and bright coffee shop. Even after an expansion, it remains true to the vision with a stone fireplace and comfy chairs. In warmer months, a large outdoor beer garden is the highlight with two large silver silos and tree shade. The place draws a local crowd and supports community nonprofits, but the brewery also distributes its beer outside Colorado.

Most of the beer names reference local places—like the massive sandstone formation **Elephant Rock**, which is the name for the piney and resinous IPA. The **Devils Head Red Ale**, a potent and spicy 7.3 percent ABV American red ale, references the mountain with the same name and its famous lookout tower. The beer menu rotates frequently but generally offers light, pale, and dark beers year-round, making it a good place to take a group of people.

In addition to the broad selection of interesting and well-executed beers, Pikes Peak serves small bites that range from beer cheese soup and flatbreads to pulled pork sliders.

TRiNiTY BREWING COMPANY

1466 Garden of the Gods Rd., Colorado Springs, CO 80907; (719) 634-0029; TrinityBrew.com
Founded: 2008 **Founder:** Jason Yester **Brewer:** Jason Yester
Flagship beers: One Ear, Seven Day Sour, Soul Horkey Ale, Sunna Wit Bier, Flo India Pale Ale, Awaken Chicory Coffee Stout, Farmhouse Saison, Slap Yer Mammy, Doodle Beer Session IPA **Seasonals/special releases:** Chocolate River, 45th Parallel IPA, Three Flowers Saison Vieille, Elektrick Cukumbahh, Super Juice Solution, Mad Ear, Menacing fruit series, Red Swingline, Oh Face, TPS Report, Damn It Feels Good to Be a Gangsta, Naked Swing, Velvet Ear, The Whole Pie, Thaison, Hopped Toddy, Saison Man, Some Weird Sin **Tours:** None **Taproom hours:** Tues through Thurs, noon to 9 p.m.; Fri, noon to 11 p.m.; Sat, 11 a.m. to 11 p.m.; Sun, 11 a.m. to 8 p.m. Bottles and crowlers to go.

Jason Yester is truly the guru and master of his domain. He's the founder and brewmaster of the colorful and much-honored TRiNiTY Brewing Company, a brewery that specializes in a dizzying number of envelope-bending saisons and adventurous and confounding Belgian sours. The operation is located in the corner lot of a business strip mall in a suburb of Colorado Springs. The liberal, slow-food eatery pours some of the most creative and unusual beers in America, and concept were embraced from the outset.

RED SWINGLINE

Style: Sour IPA
ABV: 4.1 percent
Availability: Limited release

The description of Red Swingline is intense: A 100 IBU IPA, brewed with coriander and tangerine zest and then fermented with lactobacillus and *Brettanomyces* before it is aged in French oak barrels and dry-hopped. The wild-sour hybrid is packed with pucker and flavor that is one of a kind, landing it for years on national lists of top beers.

When it opened in 2008, TRiNiTY sold out of beer within two days. While best known for his raft of outlandish saisons and sours, Yester is just as passionate about the creative selection of year-round beers at TRiNiTY, plenty of which are not sour. **Sunna Wit** is a unique take on the traditional Belgian wheat-ale style. Brewed with tangerine, lemon, and lime zests and coriander, the beer is then aged on rose petals. Sunna is also fermented with 50 percent saison yeast, which lends the quaffable and refreshing beer a soft woolly nose and a decidedly deeper and drier fruity body.

All the farmhouse saisons are brewed with a bit of Brett yeast, and one of the most popular is **One Ear**, a bright-flavored saison brewed with barley, oats, and rye that gets a light fruit and pepper character. Many of the brewery's saisons and sours are released in wax-sealed bottles that don't last long. **Elektrick Cukumbahh**, which is made with fresh local cucumbers, lemon zest, and grains of paradise, is another favorite award winner with a refreshing flavor. The menu leans toward the healthy side, which is another fresh take for a brewpub.

BREWER'S REPUBLIC

112 N. Nevada Ave., Colorado Springs, CO 80903; (719) 633-2105; BrewersRep.com
Taps: 20 **Bottles/cans:** 40+

Brewer's Republic is a craft beer haven in the heart of downtown Colorado Springs across the road from city hall. It nearly closed at one point, but the founders of Cerberus Brewing retook ownership and kept it alive.

The green exterior with a small sidewalk patio and doors plastered with beer stickers makes it an easy find. Inside, old tap handles hang from the ceiling between green metal rafter beams, and old brick walls give the place a cozy feeling. A set of padded chairs at the bar, stools in the front window, and bench seating at tables are often filled with regulars. For food, Brewer's Republic offers bar snacks, salads, sandwiches, and pizzas. The place also serves a number of Colorado craft distilleries and wine.

Most come for the beer. The 20 taps favor Colorado breweries and often include specialty kegs of brews you can't find at a typical bar or restaurant. Other breweries from across the nation—and world—pour from the other taps, including Founders and Destihl on a recent day. The styles hit the latest trends and seasons with hazy IPAs, sours, and plenty of stouts. If you don't find what you want, a dozen or so high-end bottles are available, starting around $20. The can list includes another couple dozen beers from top-notch breweries.

THE JAILHOUSE CRAFT BEER BAR

412 E. Main St., Buena Vista, CO 81211; (719) 966-5544; TheJailHouseBV.com
Taps: 10 **Bottles/cans:** 50+

The Jailhouse is unlike any craft beer bar in Colorado—and the nation. Set back from Main Street in beautiful Buena Vista, it's located in a historic jailhouse that dates to the 1880s. The walls are made with rocks that stick out on the inside and held upright by metal rods that run the length of the building. And exposed yellow lightbulbs hang from the ceiling in the dimly lit bar. The

[135]

combination gives the place a speakeasy feel with a dose of history. In addition, two patios, one out front and another in the back, offer plenty of places to enjoy the mountain air and relax with a beer.

The owner, Sarah Haughney, opened the bar in 2016 after working in the beer industry in Denver. The 10 taps offer a taste for everyone with wheats, lagers, saisons, and darker beers. The beer list constantly rotates with carefully selected options and features only independent breweries. (It's one of the few places this side of Denver you can find Bierstadt Lagerhaus, too.)

But for the beer aficionados, the bottle list is the reason to visit. It features more than three dozen rare and unique beers from the best brewers in the nation, including American Solera, Jester King, and Prairie, and covers saisons, sours, wild ales, and dark beers. The best bet: splurge on a bottle from Casey Brewing & Blending. Jailhouse is an unofficial hub for their beer and one of the few bars that carries the hard-to-find brewery from western Colorado.

TRAILS END TAPROOM

3103 W. Colorado Ave., Colorado Springs, CO 80904; (719) 428-0080; TrailsEndTaproom.com
Taps: 40

The Colorado Springs beer scene is getting more sophisticated—or at least a little more hip. Trails End Taproom offers 40 taps and lets patrons pour as much or as little as they want from each. It's like First Draft in Denver and countless others across the country. But it shows an appetite for trying different beer styles, often more interesting ones, and different breweries, including top-flight breweries from across the country and the world. Trails Ends relies heavily on scoring great kegs from Denver area breweries and a raft of national well-known beer makers. A recent menu included Ursula Brewing, High Hops, Bell's, and Left Hand.

The outdoor theme is apparent, and there's indoor space to park your bike and an outdoor patio for the dog. The location is just down US 24 from Manitou Springs on the west side of Colorado Springs across from Red Rock Canyon Open Space, a popular area for a hike or bike ride. So it's a great place for a postactivity beer or a venue for a group where everyone can find something they want to drink. The food menu is basic but will satisfy a couple cravings, with pizzas, Mountain Pie Company's meat pies, and a few appetizers.

Northwest

Aspen, Breckenridge, Carbondale, Dillon, Eagle, Frisco, Glenwood Springs, Grand Junction, and Steamboat Springs

Take the interstate west from Denver and through the tunnel under the Continental Divide to the heart of high-country Colorado with its mountains, lakes, and ski resorts. A mountain town in Colorado is not complete without its own brewery, and there are dozens of them in northwestern Colorado. The craft beer ethos and outdoor lifestyle are synonymous for most of these breweries, and you can find bikes, ski racks, and hiking boots at most these places. A handful of the region's breweries even rank among the best in the nation, making for a great pilgrimage from the city or a detour on a vacation. This region spans from Steamboat Springs in the north to Aspen on the south, Dillon in the east, and Grand Junction near the western border. Like other areas, it's impossible to mention every brewery, particularly the smaller ones that fill a thirst in their respective towns. And even this region of Colorado is seeing a surge in new breweries that are elevating the beer

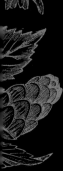

GAME, WHETHER THEY CATER TO TOURISTS WHO FLOCK TO THIS AREA OR THE LOCALS WHO LIVE ONE MOUNTAIN PASS OVER. THE REGION'S RESTAURANTS AND BARS ALSO ARE BIG SUPPORTERS OF LOCAL BEER, SO YOU CAN FIND DIFFERENT CHOICES ON TAP AT MOST PLACES.

BONFIRE BREWING

127 W. Second St., Eagle, CO 81631; (970) 306-7113; BonfireBrewing.com
Founded: 2010 **Founders:** Andy Jessen and Matt Wirtz **Brewer:** Zach Kaplan **Flagship beers:** Brush Creek Blonde Ale, Firestarter IPA, WTFO Double IPA, Demshitz Brown Ale, Kindler Pale Ale, Tent Pole Vanilla Porter **Seasonals/special releases:** Wood Splitter Pilsner, Pink-I Raspberry IPA, Coloradler, Whiskey Barrel Tent Pole **Tours:** None **Taproom hours:** Mon, 4 to 10 p.m.; Tues and Wed, noon to 10 p.m.; Thurs through Sat, noon to midnight; Sun, noon to 10 p.m. Growlers and cans to go.

Located in the small town of Eagle, Bonfire Brewing is built around the concept of a campfire, a place where people can meet and feel welcome. ("Gather 'Round" is the brewery's motto.) It started from humble beginnings. Matt Wirtz and Andy Jessen launched the brewery when they needed to make a little extra cash to cover the cost of an exiting roommate. The two avid homebrewers set about raising enough capital to go small-scale commercial. Their one investor was Jessen's father, but it was enough to get the two into a small storefront. The name came from a Web domain that Wirtz reserved for his homebrew.

Beer Lover's Pick

BRUSH CREEK BLONDE

Style: American Blonde Ale
ABV: 4.8 percent
Availability: Year-round on tap and in cans
Brewed with citrus–evoking simcoe hops, Brush Creek Blonde is a bright, sunshine-colored pour with layers of cereal malt smoothness. It is the brewery's lightest offering and a popular one for those on the mountain thanks to a lower alcohol content. The name pays tribute to the creek that provides all the water for Bonfire beer.

The Bonfire taproom pours at least 10 beers, and, like many breweries, the IPA is the most popular. **Firestarter IPA** is a 6.6 percent ABV American IPA brewed and dry-hopped with amarillo, centennial, and loral hops. The **Demshitz Brown Ale**, named for a group of local kayakers, is darker and more roasted than most in the category with an earthy hop note, essentially making it a richer version than others. Jessen describes his beer as being built for the Everyman, and the brewery doesn't specialize in a particular style, instead trying to do most well.

The brewers joke that a 45-second self-guided tour of the brewery operations is available, but the place recently expanded its space with a patio. Most of their production in cans is done off-site at a different facility and available at nearby liquor stores.

BROKEN COMPASS BREWING COMPANY

68 Continental Ct., Breckenridge, CO 80424; (970) 368-2772; BrokenCompassBrewing.com
Founded: 2014 **Founders:** David Axelrod and Jason Ford **Brewer:** Jason Ford **Flagship beers:** Czech Pilsner, Irish Red, Ginger Pale Ale, Chili Pepper Pale Ale, Centennial IPA, Double IPA, Coconut Porter, Imperial Bourbon Brown **Seasonals/special releases:** Hefeweizen, The Winchester, Chocolate Coffee Stout, Wet Hop IPA, Wild Peach Pale **Tours:** None **Taproom hours:** Mon through Sun, 11 a.m. to 10 p.m. Bottles and growlers to go.

The original Breckenridge Brewery is probably the best known in this ski town, but the locals drink at Broken Compass down the road. The brewery is located in an industrial park a couple miles north of the tourist-filled sidewalks and downtown hubbub but not far off SR 9, the main route to the skiing, mountain biking, and hiking that makes Breckenridge a top destination.

David Axelrod and Jason Ford founded the company, but the two partners later split. Axelrod opened his own place in nearby Frisco. Ford, a chemical engineer by training, still makes the beer and relishes the intimate experience at Broken Compass. In the middle of the taproom, an old chairlift serves as bench seating between picnic tables. More than a dozen beers pour at the bar, which is framed by blonde wood rafters. A side patio is where the mud-speckled mountain bikers sit after long rides. The place is dog- and kid-friendly and maintains a low-key atmosphere. No food is served, but you can bring your own.

The beer list shifts with the seasons, featuring hefeweizen and Czech pilsners in the summer, wet-hopped beers in the fall, and darker stouts in the winter. The brewery is probably best known for its **Coconut Porter**, a robust porter with roasted coconut that is sweet but not too much. The **Ginger Pale Ale** and **Chili Pepper Pale Ale** are two more mainstays that take fun diversions on a traditional style. Once you get off the mountain, avoid the crowds at the base and the hordes downtown to join the locals for après in this cozy taproom.

CASEY BREWING & BLENDING

3421 Grand Ave., Glenwood Springs, CO 81601; (970) 230-9691; CaseyBrewing.com
Founded: 2013 **Founder:** Troy Casey **Brewers:** Troy Casey and Eric Metzger **Flagship beers:** Saison, Oak Theory, Fruit Stand series, The Cut series, Casey Family Preserves series **Seasonal/special releases:** Advanced Oak Theory, Jammy, Leaner, Biere de Garde, Brett Loves series, East Bank, The Low End, The Mix, Funky Blender series **Tours:** By online appointment, ticket required **Taproom hours:** By online appointment only. Bottles to go.

The most coveted beers in Colorado are made on the banks of the Roaring Fork River in Glenwood Springs. Casey Brewing & Blending came to life in 2013 after founder Troy Casey left his job at AC Golden, the Coors subsidiary in Golden, and decided to open a brewery dedicated to farmhouse and wild ales in this remote outpost in western Colorado.

He found a passion in an Old World process, making oak-aged beers aged with a blend of yeast, *Brettanomyces*, and lactic acid bacteria, and added flair with doses of local fruit, like apricots, plums, raspberries, cherries, and more. The beers are made with almost all Colorado ingredients.

The huge interest from the beer community initially overwhelmed the operation with devotees driving across state lines and sleeping in their cars to arrive early to snag one of the precious bottles. The demand remains, but Casey transitioned the brewery to a winery model with scheduled tours and

Beer Lover's Pick

PEACH CASEY FAMILY PRESERVES

Style: Saison
ABV: 6 percent
Availability: Limited

Colorado is known for its Palisade peaches grown on the Western Slope. The sweet and ripe fruit is an annual treat. And Casey Brewing & Blending pays homage in a series of beers each year. The Peach Casey Family Preserves starts as a mixed-culture saison and then gets aged on more than two pounds of peaches per gallon of beer. Casey releases multiple editions featuring different peach varieties that showcase the range of flavors in the fruit that emerge in the aging process.

tastings at set times Thursdays through Sundays. A ticket is required to visit and drink at the taproom, but the intimate experience is worth it and allows visitors to really learn how the beer is made. The ticket price is applied to the cost of the beers.

The beers—which you can find in select beer bars and beer stores (see Appendix)—represent traditional styles, such as the Belgian-style sour series **Oak Theory**, a farmhouse ale with honey called **East Bank**, and a traditional **Saison**. The fruited beers are a big draw. The **Fruit Stand** series or the more intense **Casey Family Preserves**, both saisons, showcase the different varieties of fruit and the delicate interplay with the mixed-culture fermentation. But pretty much any beer you taste will show the depth and complexity Casey is known to create.

OUTER RANGE BREWING COMPANY

182 Lusher Ct., Frisco, CO 80443; (970) 455-8709; OuterRange.com
Founded: 2016 **Founders:** Emily and Lee Cleghorn **Brewer:** Lee Cleghorn **Flagship beers:** Outer Range IPA, Final Summit **Seasonals/special releases:** In the Steep, Forestry, Blocks of Light, Corduroy, In the Deep Steep, Orb Table Bierre, Luminous Flux, Wunkerkind **Tours:** None **Taproom hours:** Mon through Thurs, 3 to 10 p.m.; Fri and Sat, noon to 11 p.m.; Sun, noon to 10 p.m. Cans to go.

Northwest

Outer Range Brewing mainly makes two styles of beer: IPAs and Belgians. It sounds limiting until you see a beer menu with a dozen-plus choices, all different expressions of the main styles. What Outer Range is best known for is even more specific: hazy IPAs. It's become a destination and draws crowds from down the mountain for its can releases.

The husband-and-wife team behind the brewery took its name from a Richard Kipling poem and embraces the idea of brewing at 9,075 feet. Frisco is situated in a bend of I-70, a gateway to the town of Breckenridge, where it is ringed by mountains that are visible through a large garage door that opens into a courtyard in the summer. In the winter months, the brewery erects a yurt in the courtyard to make room for additional warm seating—one of the more unique beer-tasting experiences in Colorado.

The 15-barrel brew house in a shopping center uses the turbid New England–style IPA as a playground for hops, mixing different varieties in endless combinations. The hops give the beer a range of flavors from savory to sweet, and some editions are refined and others more blunt. The **In the Steep** IPA and its bolder cousin, **In the Deep Steep** double IPA, are two of the better-rated beers with big hop flavor and a huge dry-hop aroma. On the Belgian side, **Final Summit** is a French saison with a round mouthfeel that manages to finish delicately dry and crisp.

Beer Lover's Pick

IN THE STEEP

Style: Hazy IPA
ABV: 6.7 percent
Availability: Year-round on draft and in limited edition cans

Like most hazy IPAs, In the Steep pours like juice. It looks like Sunny D, to be more exact, a completely opaque yellow-orange color that is loaded with hop flavors. The beer dons different hop editions, but the citra and Nelson sauvin version starts with tropical and citrus flavors and finishes with bitterness, a reminder that it's still an IPA and not really juice. Look for dry-hopped editions for an extra punch.

ROARING FORK BEER COMPANY

358 Main St., Carbondale, CO 81623; (970) 510-5934;
RoaringForkBeerCo.com
Founded: 2013 **Founder:** Chase Engel **Brewers:** Chase Engel and
Dodge Cottle **Flagship beers:** Slaughterhouse Lager and Freestone
Extra Pale Ale **Seasonals/special releases:** Oktoberfest, Emma
Hibiscus Rose, Fat Pagan Barleywine, New Pattern Double IPA, Triple
Flip, Roll Session Blonde, Street Cred **Tours:** By appointment **Taproom
hours:** Mon through Thurs, 3 to 10 p.m.; Fri and Sat, 2 to 11 p.m.

Carbondale is located between the towns of Glenwood Springs to the north
and Aspen to the south, and it's a place known for its outdoor recreation
opportunities. The business district is just off the main highway, and makes for
a nice stop after a day of skiing or mountain biking.

Roaring Fork Beer Company pours its beers at Batch, a tasting room in
the heart of downtown Carbondale, making it a community-centered space. It
hosts a number of nonprofits and artists for special events at the tasting room.
The brewery decided to move out of its production facility and into a century-
old building downtown about four years after it opened. The move made
more room for beer making and beer tasting. The brewery now packages and
distributes to much of the state and expects more expansion to come.

The new place takes on a varied feel, from living room to Texas speakeasy,
which is a nod toward the founder's roots. It holds two dozen taps, as compared
to the six at the original Dolores Way production facility. Batch also serves food
and pours guest taps as well as wine and other craft beverages from Colorado
companies. The brewery focuses on making what it calls "seasonally inspired
beers," so it debuts new ones each season. The **Freestone Extra Pale Ale**
is the place to start.

STORM PEAK BREWING COMPANY

1885 Elk River Plaza, Steamboat Springs, CO; (970) 879-
1999; StormPeakBrewing.com
Founded: 2014 **Founders:** Tyler and Wyatt Patterson **Brewers:**
Tyler and Wyatt Patterson **Flagship beers:** Lawnmower, Mad Creek,
Gaper, 4 Wire, Maestro, Chowder, Coffee Moos **Seasonals/special
releases:** The Arborist, Mr. Night, Flare, Regency, Do You Respect

Wood, Yukon Stout **Tours:** None **Taproom hours:** Mon through Sun, noon to 10 p.m. Growlers, bottles, crowlers, and cans to go.

Steamboat Springs didn't even get a mention in the Colorado beer world not long ago, but now it's home to a handful of craft breweries that make a great destination after a day outdoors. Storm Peak Brewing is a good place to see the experimentation and boundary pushing in the local beer market. It's also located half a mile south on Elk River Road from the award-winning Butcherknife Brewing Company, making for a nice combination tour.

Storm Peak is the product of brother duo Tyler and Wyatt Patterson, who started as homebrewers. The pair looked at space in Denver but decided to land in Steamboat Springs because the market was less crowded. Within a few years, the brewery's popularity forced the brothers to abandon the original location and move to its current place with more room for production. It's now canning and bottling a number of its beers, too. The locals followed and give the place a chill feel where people seem to know one another.

The 20 taps constantly rotate, and a handful of bright spots emerge. The **Lawnmower** beer, a cream ale, gets an extra dose of hops at the end to give it a twist, and different versions are released often. The **Coffee Moos**, a coffee milk stout, is one of the standbys with rich flavors that fit the cool summer evenings and snowy winters alike.

Beer Lover's Pick

SERENITY NOW
Style: Kettle Sour
ABV: 5.8 percent
Availability: Limited on draft
Kettle sours are too often face-puckering tart, a one-note edition of the style without the nuance of a barrel-aged version. Not so with Serenity Now, a sour red ale with plums. This beer is loaded with 850 pounds of plum puree and soured with Greek yogurt for a refreshing beer with depth. The plums develop stone-fruit and earthy tones that meld well with the tartness and add to the gorgeous red hue.

BREWPUBS

GLENWOOD CANYON BREWING COMPANY

402 7th St., Glenwood Springs, CO 81601; (970) 945-1276;
GlenwoodCanyon.com
Founded: 1996 **Founders:** Steve and April Carver **Brewers:** Todd
Malloy and Cody Nelson **Flagship beers:** Alpha-Beta Project, Grizzly
Creek Raspberry Wheat, Hanging Lake Honey Ale, St. James Irish Red
Ale, Vapor Cave IPA **Seasonals/special releases:** Strawberry Daze,
Anticline Altbier, Barrel Project, Dotsero Cream Ale, Zephyr Hefeweizen,
100 Star Pre-prohibition Pilsner, 7th Street Irish Stout, Carbonator
Doppelbock, No Name Nut Brown Ale, Shoshone Stout, Canyon Trail
American Pale Ale, Forest Hallow Pumpkin Ale **Tours:** None **Taproom
hours:** Mon through Sun, 11 a.m. to 10 p.m. Growlers and cans to go.

The first brewery in Glenwood Springs arrived in 1914 with the appropriate name Home Brewing Company. A fire and Prohibition put it out of business two years later. But just blocks from the original brewery's location, Glenwood Canyon Brewing is keeping the tradition alive. Born in the 1990s brewpub boom, the brewery is located in bottom of the Hotel Denver in the town's Riverfront district across the street from a railroad depot built in 1904 that is still in operation.

Glenwood Canyon is the place to find true-to-style beers, and it's the most awarded brewery in western Colorado with two dozen or so major competition medals from 2001 to 2018. The 12 taps include five year-round beers, four rotating seasonals, two guest sours, and a guest cider. If you want to find well-executed beers, try the **St. James Irish Red Ale**, the **No Name Nut Brown Ale**, or the **Shoshone Stout**. For the hop lover, there is **Vapor Cave IPA**, an abundantly bittered pale that has layers of green herbal bite and lively pine-needle aroma. All are award winners.

The brewery sticks to specific styles rather than blur the lines with experimentation and funky beers, but if you arrive during the annual Strawberry Days Festival in June, you can try the brewpub's special beer for the event. **Strawberry Daze** is an American amber ale that is brewed with 300 pounds per batch of strawberries.

In addition to the beer, the pub menu offers classic appetizers, salads, soups, stews, burgers, sandwiches, pastas, fish-and-chips, pizzas, and steaks.

KANNAH CREEK BREWING COMPANY

1960 N. 12th St., Grand Junction, CO 81501; (970) 263-0111;
KannahCreekBrewingCo.com
905 Struthers Ave., Grand Junction, CO 81501; (970) 243-3659
Founded: 2005 **Founders:** Bernadette and Jim Jeffryes **Brewer:**
Jim Jeffryes **Flagship beers:** Black's Bridge Stout, Broken Oar IPA,
Highside Hefeweizen, Island Mesa Blonde, Lands End Amber, Pigasus
Porter, Standing Wave Pale Ale **Seasonals/special releases:**
Bahaa Nieche, The Nightroweizen, Doppelbock, Schwartzbier, Maibock,
Edgewater Altbier, Hoch Hopfen, Edgewater Kolsch, Pilsner, Cherry
Bourbon Barrel Brown **Tours:** None **Taproom hours:** Sun through
Thurs, 11 a.m. to 10 p.m.; Fri and Sat, 11 a.m. to 11 p.m.

The city of Grand Junction, on Colorado's expansive Western Slope, is
better known for its wine and fruit than its brew-savvy, but Kannah Creek
Brewing is changing that perception with familiar styles of beer. The founder,
former tech industry employee and homebrewer Jim Jeffryes, decided to open
a brewery after being diagnosed with multiple sclerosis.

Kannah Creek now operates two locations, and each pours different
beer and serves different food. The original on 12th Street, dubbed The
Creek, houses a small brewing system that allows the restaurant's 13 taps to
consistently rotate. The second location, known as Edgewater, sits a couple
miles away on a three-acre property along the Colorado River in an emerging

part of town. Responding to the increasingly crowded craft beer market, Kannah Creek recently went through a reinvention of itself and sold its big brewing system at the Edgewater location to downsize and focus on making lagers. The revamp also leaves room for a bigger kitchen, more seating, and event space.

The food menu at the Edgewater location covers the basics with appetizers like nachos, burgers and brats, and various sandwiches, but the Creek pub specializes in pizzas, pastas, and calzones. The beer covers a range of traditional styles. **Black's Bridge Stout** is a bold, chocolate brown–colored pour, served like Guinness on a nitrogen tap to give it a smooth, creamy body and thick, fluffy head. The roasty beer has deep notes of freshly brewed coffee, charcoal, and bitter baker's chocolate. **Broken Oar IPA** is brewed more in the maltier English model with layers of pine-needle and yellow citrus fruit depth, with notes of sweet tropical fruit.

MOUNTAIN TAP BREWERY

910 Yampa St., #103, Steamboat Springs, CO 80487; (970) 879-6646; MountainTapBrewery.com
Founded: 2016 **Founders:** Rich and Wendy Tucciarone **Brewer:** Rich Tucciarone **Flagship beers:** Locals' Lager, Passionate Pedal, Picking Hops IPA, Current IPA, Chasing Sunset Golden Ale, Paddlers' Porter, Cliffed Out **Seasonals/special releases:** Summer Heat Ginger Wheat, Zwickel, Passionate Pedal, Get Out!, Nitro Hop, Camp Clean, Livin' the Steam, Mountain Macaroon, MacaRUM, Halaboration River Pale Ale, Summer Haze IPA, Makin' Hay Double IPA, Fall Line, Downtown Ginger Brown, Rendezvous Red, Routty Red **Tours:** None **Taproom hours:** Tues through Thurs, 3:30 to 9 p.m.; Fri and Sat, 3:30 to 10 p.m.; Sun, 3:30 to 9 p.m. Growlers and crowlers to go.

In downtown Steamboat Springs, a block away from the busy sidewalks of Lincoln Avenue, you can find one of the state's most experienced brewers. Mountain Tap Brewery's Rich Tucciarone spent five years at Breckenridge Brewery, where he served as head brewer, and then another 12 years leading brewing operations for Kona Brewing Company in Hawaii. Soon after returning to the Yampa Valley, he opened his own place.

Mountain Tap Brewery pours 12 taps and keeps the lines fresh with different styles. The first beer Tucciarone made is **Picking Hops**, a bolder, dry-hopped version of the **Current IPA** that is big on citrus and pine, so it's a good place to start at the bar. The **Mountain Macaroon** is one of the more interesting beers on the menu. It starts as a malty brown ale and then gets aged on toasted coconut to make it taste like a little treat. The flavors only get bigger and sweeter in **MacaRUM**, a version that is aged on rum-soaked oak for several weeks.

The brewery is situated across the street from the Yampa River, where a walking trail offers a nice stroll. In the summer, Mountain Tap opens the garage doors and looks like an outdoor bazaar with dogs tied up on the sidewalk and bikes leaning against oak barrels out front. The menu offers wood-fired pizzas, along with snacks and salads. The place just captures the town's laid-back vibe.

CRAFTSMAN VAIL

56 Edwards Village Blvd., Unit 112, Edwards, CO 81632;
(970) 926-5833; CraftsmanVail.com
Taps: 12 Bottles/cans: 15

Keep taking I-70 west from Vail and Beaver Creek ski resorts to the town of Edwards, where you can find Craftsman Vail, a boutique sandwich shop with a great craft beer menu. It may seem out of the way for travelers from Denver, but it's worth the extra mileage to break free from the monotony that awaits at the base of most resorts.

The tap handles don't cover the entire wall, but the 12 options are thoughtfully selected to include a number of hip breweries and fun styles, including the likes of TRVE, Cerebral, Jester King, and others. The Craftsman crew even travels to pick up kegs from breweries that don't distribute widely, meaning you can find beers that don't typically make it to these parts of the mountains. Also keep an eye out for other local breweries, such as Vail Brewing Company.

It's a deluxe dining and beer experience but in a casual setting, so you can visit in muddy trail runners or ski pants. The food menu rotates like the beer list. But recent options included shaved pork belly, olive tapenade, arugula, tomato, and mayo on a toasted baguette; a poke bowl with salmon belly and guacamole; and a torta with Colorado Lamb chorizo, fried green tomato, roasted chili aioli, provolone, and shredded lettuce.

HOPS CULTURE

414 E. Hyman Ave., Aspen, CO 81611; (970) 925-4677;
HopsCulture.com
Taps: 30 Bottles/cans: 200+

Down the stairs, tucked away on the Hyman Avenue pedestrian mall in downtown Aspen, sits a craft beer bar with so many great options that you'll question whether it's worth getting up early for first tracks on the ski hill the next morning.

Hops Culture pours 30 beers from draft and features a bottle and can list as large as a book, covering all range of styles and a number of limited releases.

All the great options make it difficult to pick from the L-shaped tapwall or the bright beer fridge. But the bartenders will make it easy on you, offering their favorite picks of the moment and a tasting flight so you can cover more ground.

On the beer menu, look for the local favorites, Roaring Fork Brewing Company from Carbondale or Aspen Brewing Company, the latter of which operates their own Aspen Tap a block away on South Galena Street. Or hit the big highlights from national breweries like Russian River, The Bruery, Port, and Dogfish Head.

If you want to people watch, sit at one of the street-side stools otherwise tuck yourself in a corner booth downstairs to stay a spell. The elevated comfort-food menu pairs well with the beer options. The cheese curds are served with a side of stout beer ranch dip, and the nachos come with house-made chips and wild boar carnitas. For dessert, you can make table-side roasted s'mores to pair with a rich stout.

Southwest
Cortez, Del Norte, Dolores, Durango, Gunnison, Montrose, Ouray, Pagosa Springs, Ridgway, and Telluride

In southwestern Colorado, you will find great views and great brews. This part of the state is magnificent for its massive peaks, natural monuments, and huge scale. It's a lengthy road trip from the Denver area, where most come and go from Colorado, but worth the time to explore. Like the Northwest region, many of these remote outposts and adventure towns include a brewery (if not two). Even if the names didn't make the book, it's still fun to stop and try the local brews and get a flavor for the area. A couple of the state's oldest and best brewers are found in this region, as are some of the most unique. Durango is home to one of the most established brewing scenes thanks to Carver Brewpub, the second oldest in the state. And without the groundbreaking efforts of brewpubs in these small towns, it is doubtful whether the craft beer movement in Colorado would have gained the momentum it has enjoyed since the early 1990s. Now

THE REGION IS HOME TO TRENDSETTER BREWERIES LIKE SKA AND TELLURIDE. NEXT TIME YOU ARE THINKING OF TAKING A ROAD TRIP IN COLORADO OR, INDEED, IF YOU'RE LOOKING FOR OFF-THE-BEATEN-PATH BREWERIES TO VISIT, YOU'D BE WISE TO CONSIDER SOUTHWESTERN COLORADO.

SKA BREWING COMPANY

225 Girard St., Durango, CO 81303; (970) 247-5792; SkaBrewing.com
Founded: 1995 **Founders:** Bill Graham and Dave Thibodeau **Brewer:** Bill Graham **Flagship beers:** True Blonde Ale, Rue B. Soho, Pink Vapor Stew, Moral Panic Brut IPA, Modus Hoperandi IPA, Modus Mandarina IPA, Rudie Session IPA, BHC DIPA, Pinstripe Red Ale, Buster Nut Brown Ale, Steel Toe Stout **Seasonals/special releases:** Mexican Logger, Sour Apple Gose, Tart Mexican Logger, Euphoria Pale Ale, Decadent Imperial IPA, Oktoberfest, MoSka Mule, Autumnal Mole Stout **Tours:** Mon through Sat, 4 p.m. **Taproom hours:** Mon through Fri, 9 a.m. to 9 p.m.; Sat 11 a.m. to 9 p.m.; Sun, 11 a.m. to 7 p.m. Growlers, bottles, and cans to go.

Ska Brewing Company is the largest brewery in southwestern Colorado, and its beers travel to a dozen states. Founded in 1995 by Bill Graham and Dave Thibodeau, Ska was named after the jaunty music of the same name that they loved so much. There is an irreverent and sassy vibe about the beers brewed by Ska. This can be partly attributed to the colorful comic-book characters that are posed and emblazoned on every label. The characters are

Ska Brewing Company

lifted from an unpublished comic book that Bill, Dave, and a friend created while in college. New characters appear with the release of new beers, and each character has an interrelated backstory.

Ska was the second craft brewery in the nation to can its beer. IPAs fill the beer list, with **Moral Panic Brut IPA** one of the newest and **Modus Hoperandi IPA** one of its standbys. The shining copper-colored ale is a complex hop bomb with a brilliant sappy pine aroma and a bitter, sticky body. Notes of sage, pine, and lime peel are all present and accounted for in a beer with significant bitterness that doesn't overwhelm.

Beer Lover's Pick

OKTOBERFEST
Style: German-Style Lager
ABV: 6.1 percent
Availability: Fall seasonal

Unlike so many modern beers, Oktoberfest lagers highlight the nuances of malt and let the yeast and hops play a minor supporting role. This award-winning version is one of the more flavorful in the category, pouring an amber color with flavors of nuts and bread crust from the toasted Munich and Vienna malts. The crisp lager taste matches the cool air when this beer debuts in Durango.

The brewery's innovation is on display at its "World Headquarters," as its owners call the home base, in an industrial park outside downtown Durango. One beer that went from the brewery experiment series known as the Mod Project to year-round beer is **Pink Vapor Stew**. The sour is made with beets, carrots, ginger, and apples, along with citra and belma hops to deliver a surprisingly tasty brew.

TELLURIDE BREWING COMPANY

156 Society Dr., Telluride, CO 81435; (970) 728-5094; TellurideBrewingCo.com
Founded: 2012 **Founders:** Chris Fish, Tommy Thacher, Brian Gavin, and John Lehman **Brewer:** Chris Fish **Flagship beers:** Bridal Veil Rye Pale Ale, Russell Kelly Pale Ale, Face Down Brown, Whacked Out Wheat, Tempter IPA, Fishwater Double IPA **Seasonals/special releases:** Freaky Fish, redFISH Ale, Tripel in Stillwater, Beaver Pond Blonde, Dank in the Dark, Greensky American Lager, Señor Gomez, Ski-in-Ski-Stout, There Gose the Snow, Face Down Bourbon Brown, Fishwater Project, Freaky Cab, Freaquila, Tripel Cork, Tripel Show **Tours:** None **Taproom hours:** Mon through Sun, noon to 8 p.m. Growlers and cans to go.

Outdoor sports, the Grateful Dead, and good local beer brought together the cofounders of Telluride Brewing Company, Chris Fish and Tommy Thacher. At the time, Fish was already a award-winning brewmaster, and Thacher was a bartender. The pair joined forces with Brian Gavin, a real estate

Beer Lover's Pick

GREENSKY AMERICAN LAGER
Style: American Lager
ABV: 5.2 percent
Availability: Seasonal on tap and in cans
Named for the famed bluegrass band, Telluride Brewing Company's Greensky American Lager is the beer you can drink all day long at a music festival. It's crisp with a traditional malt flavor but spiked with a punch of mosaic hops that makes it a fun and modern take on the style. It's a lively beer that hits all the best notes, much like the band.

broker, and John Lehman, a local artist, to give their dream and business plan more viability, and the four opened Telluride Brewing, which poured its first beer in 2012. The brewery is located on the way into town at the base of a box canyon, making it a great stop on the way to the many summer music and film festivals or the ski resort.

Telluride makes a well-rounded selection of core styles year-round with a flair for Belgian styles in its limited-release beers. The **Face Down Brown** ale is the epitome of the category with toffee and chocolate notes. **Tempter IPA** is brewed with six varieties of hops and delivers a bold herbaceous aroma from the dry-hop. The **Ski-in-Ski-Stout** is a dessert-friendly, chocolate-forward American stout with moderate bitterness and a full mouthfeel.

The barrel-aged beers take it one step further. The **Freaky Cab**, a rare edition released a couple times a year, is the **Fishwater Double IPA** brewed with a strong ale yeast that is double dry-hopped and aged in Cabernet Sauvignon barrels for a year.

CARVER BREWING COMPANY

1022 Main Ave., Durango, CO 81301; (970) 259-2545; Carver Brewing.com
Founded: 1988 **Founders:** Jim Carver, Bill Carver, and Barb Wynne
Brewers: Patrick Jose and Cody Looman **Flagship beers:** Jack Rabbit Pale Ale, Old Oak Amber Ale, Lightner Creek Lager, Colorado Trail Nut Brown Ale, Raspberry Wheat Ale **Seasonals/special releases:** La Plata Pilsner, Munich Dunkel, Oktoberfest Lager, The Swartz, Cerveza Real Lager, Garden Brauc Hefeweizen, Double Pepper Saison, Belgian Dubbel, Twilight Peak IPA, Big Bike Double IPA, Iron Horse Oatmeal Stout, Power House Porter, Smoked Baltic Porter, Imperial Stout, Irish Stout **Tours:** None **Taproom hours:** Sun through Thurs, 7 a.m. to 9 p.m.; Fri and Sat, 7 a.m. to 10 p.m.

Carver Brewing Company in the southwestern Colorado town of Durango prides itself on local firsts. When it opened in 1988, it was the first brewery in the entire Four Corners region since Prohibition and only the second brewpub in the state.

It remains an anchor in downtown Durango's Main Street, open breakfast to dinner with a standard menu designed to please the whole family. The restaurant offers a little bit of everything with a bar at the front of the house and a little nook that looks onto the street. In the back is a mini brewpub with views of the steel tanks and another bar, and then out back is a large patio area known as the beer garden. The water is heated by solar collectors on the roof, and the brewery is 100 percent wind powered.

Brewer Patrick Jose has a passion for European lagers because the styles are so clean that there's no place to hide imperfections. The **Lightner Creek Lager** is the prototypical dad beer, akin to Pabst Blue Ribbon but with a craft vibe and more flavor. And the **La Plata Pilsner** is a hoppier example of the style with a light biscuit-malt profile for the summer months.

The **Jack Rabbit Pale Ale** is a Carver staple that hopheads should sample. The sunshine-colored pour is loaded with spritzy citrus and fresh grassy notes, and the bitterness is even with the medium-dry finish. Served on nitrogen, **Iron Horse Oatmeal Stout** is a robust roast-forward American oatmeal stout with a moderate to high hop-derived bitterness. The oatmeal makes for a requisitely smooth sip, and serving a beer on nitrogen lends it creamy texture.

COLORADO BOY PUB BREWING COMPANY

602 Clinton St., Ridgway, CO 81432; (970) 626-5333; ColoradoBoy.com; Taproom hours: Mon through Fri, 4 to 9 p.m.; Sat and Sun, noon to 9 p.m.
320 E. Main St., Montrose, CO 81401; (970) 240-2790; Taproom hours: Tues through Sun, 11:30 a.m. to 9 p.m.
Founded: 2007 Founders: Sandy and Tom Hennessy Brewer: Elliott Bell Flagship beers: Irish Ale, Pale Ale, Blonde Seasonals/special releases: Colorado Boy IPA, Porter, Best Bitter, Brown Tours: None. Growlers and crowlers to go.

There is no shortage of entrepreneurial spirit in American craft beer, but even in an industry of dreamers and executors, Tom Hennessy stands tall. Over the years, Tom has opened, run, and sold five different breweries in New Mexico and Colorado. In 2007, he opened his sixth, Colorado Boy Pub & Brewery, which he hopes will be his last and most remembered brewing venture. He also helped countless other brewers start their businesses with his custom immersion program that takes a pair of partners through the brewing process and business.

The original Colorado Boy is located in a 100-year-old building on a main street in the small town of Ridgway on Colorado's Western Slope, where the roads weren't even paved until a few years ago. The small, 25-seat brewpub offers up a focused selection of core styles and a small menu of pizzas. He opened another location in Montrose before selling the enterprise to a former brewing student.

The beers are classic, and the menu isn't long, but finding to-style beers in a small town like this is a treat. **Irish Ale**, an award winner, is a bold Irish red ale with a rich toffee caramel character, low bitterness, and a biscuit finish. Another British-inspired trait of Colorado Boy is the ongoing presentation of a beer that has been cask conditioned. The likes of the malt-forward house **Best Bitter** benefit greatly from this method of finishing, much more so than being forced carbonated.

DOLORES RIVER BREWERY

100 N. 4th St., Dolores, CO 81323; (970) 882-4677; Dolores
RiverBrewery.com
Founded: 2002 **Founder:** Mark Youngquist **Brewers:** Mark Youngquist
and Andy Lewis **Flagship beers:** Pale Ale, ESB, American Cream
Ale, Snaggletooth Double IPA **Seasonals/special releases:** Sweet
Jamaican Brown Ale, Class V IPA, Krampas, Irish Red Ale, Young American
Pilsner **Tours:** None **Taproom hours:** Tues through Sun, 4 to 11 p.m.

One of the state's most accomplished brewers is located in one of the
state's most remote towns, Dolores. Mark Youngquist, the founder of
Dolores River Brewery, started in 1986 at BridgePort in Portland, Oregon, and
later helped found the now ubiquitous Rock Bottom Brewery.

Unlike his former employers, Youngquist prides himself on not brewing to
style. Walk into his tiny, unique taproom, and you'll find beers of familiar styles,
like an English Extra Special Bitter or an American pale ale, being poured
alongside beers like Liquid Sunshine, an IPA-modeled beer. He's particularly
interested in Old World lagers.

Dolores River has a local, community-centric vibe with a boost from
travelers who visit the nearby Canyon of the Ancients or Mesa Verde National
Park. It's also a hub for great mountain biking. Youngquist doesn't distribute his
beers widely or enter competitions, so you need to travel here to find them. But
the brewery does can small batches of some of its beers.

An expansion added space for a beer garden and room for live music, a
special emphasis for the brewery, which lures an impressive roster of bands.
The extra room also allowed for a brew lab that will give Dolores River a chance
to do barrel aging and expand its style sheet. On the food side, the brewery
specializes in wood-fired pizza, made in a home-built oven.

HIGH ALPINE BREWING COMPANY

111 North Main St., Gunnison, CO 81230; (970) 642-4500;
highalpinebrewing.com
Founded: 2015 **Founders:** Jon Brown and Scott Cline **Brewers:**
Scott Cline and Nick Lawson **Flagship beers:** Gunny Gold Kölsch,
Anthracite Amber Ale, Green Gate IPA **Seasonals/special releases:**
The Matron, Old Crank Barleywine, Sol's Espresso Stout, Aberdeen
Chocolate Maple Porter, Wildcraft series **Tours:** None **Taproom
hours:** Sun through Thurs, 11 a.m. to 11 p.m.; Fri through Sat, 11 a.m. to
midnight. Growlers and crowlers to go.

Southwest

High Alpine's slogan is "where beer meets treeline," and it's fitting for the brewery at 7,703 feet in the heart of the Colorado mountains. Located in an old brick building on Gunnison's main street, the brewery is situated at an adventure crossroads. The small college town is the gateway to Crested Butte to the north and sits between Monarch Pass and the Blue Mesa Reservoir.

In other words, the perfect location for a brewery and restaurant. The upstairs porch overlooking main street is the best seat when it's nice outside. Inside, the tall ceilings and wood rafters make room for a loft with tables and the main level features a bar made with reclaimed wood. The feel is part saloon, part restaurant. High Alpine covers the basics with its tap list, from the light **Gunny Gold Kölsch** to the **Matron**, a barrel-aged stout. All hit the spot for a weary traveler. In the winter, the **Aberdeen Chocolate Maple Porter** is subtle and easy drinking with only a limited dash of maple sweetness.

The brewery serves an elevated menu with burrata and steamed mussels to complement the salads, sandwiches and brick-oven pizzas. Each pizza is listed with a beer pairing, and the pig n' fig is nicely matched with the Anthracite Amber.

OURAY BREWING

607 Main St., Ouray, CO 81427; (970) 325-7388; Ouray Brewery.com
Founded: 2010 **Founders:** Pacie and Erin Eddy **Brewer:** Erin Eddy **Flagship beers:** Alpine Amber, Honey Rye, 550 Red Ale, Box Canyon Brown Ale, Camp Bird Blonde, Bluegrass Pale Ale, San Juan IPA **Seasonals/special releases:** Summer Saison, Silvershield Stout, Batch One IPA, Desperado Imperial Red, Kayle's Scottish Ale, Stormy's Imperial Stout, Portland Porter **Tours:** None **Taproom hours:** Mon through Sun, 11 a.m. to 9 p.m. Crowlers to go.

Ouray is one of the most picturesque Colorado mountain towns. It's situated along the Million Dollar Highway, a spectacular drive on sheer cliffs without guardrails where the road seems to hang on the mountainside and offers impressive vistas.

The three-story, family-owned brewpub Ouray Brewing offers plenty of seating, and it's often packed with tourists in the summer and a solid crowd of hearty locals in the shoulder seasons. The reason to visit Ouray Brewing is the rooftop deck, which surely ranks as one of the best places to drink beer in Colorado on a sunny, warm afternoon. It offers great views of the mountainside and nearby peaks, not to mention the Fourth of July festivities downtown.

The core beers are solid, and the seasonals add more color to the menu. **Camp Bird Blonde** is like any good, hay-colored, American blonde ale, an easy-drinking affair. **Box Canyon Brown Ale** has medium bitterness and soft residual biscuit sweetness. The nose has inviting notes of English toffee, mocha, and hazelnut. For hop lovers, **San Juan IPA** will be the no-brainer, go-to choice at Ouray. This American-style IPA has a big citrus and tropical fruit profile. **Silvershield Stout** is a strong inky stout with a thick, dark-chocolate aroma, a bitter cocoa and espresso body, and a roasted cocoa nib and licorice finish.

The buffalo wings are a highlight on the food menu, along with the house-smoked chicken sandwich called Chuck Norris. The remainder of the menu is salads and burgers, all in the model of classic pub food.

RIFF RAFF BREWING COMPANY

274 Pagosa St., Pagosa Springs, CO 81147; (970) 264-4677; RiffRaffBrewing.com
Founded: 2013 **Founders:** Randy and Eleanor Schnose and Jason and Shelly Cox **Brewer:** Randy Schnose **Flagship beers:** Hopgoblin American IPA, Man's Best Friend Honey Kölsch, Plebeian Porter, Skallywag English Pale, Stepchild American Red, El Duende Green Chile Ale **Seasonals/special releases:** Sut's Faux-Kanee American Lager, Spirited Lass Strong Scotch Ale, The Oatlaw Coffee Oatmeal Stout, Weapon of Self Destruction Russian Imperial Stout, Black Cherry Porter, 99 Shilling Scottish Ale, Holy Schnitzel Doppelbock, Not-Sober-Fest Oktoberfest, Cranberry Spruce Juice Ale **Tours:** None **Taproom hours:** Mon through Sun, 11 a.m. to 10 p.m.

The quaint town of Pagosa Springs is known for its geothermal hot springs, which fill small and large pools and draw visitors from across the world. The town is home to the world's deepest geothermal hot spring, in fact, at 1,002 feet. Riff Raff Brewing uses the geothermal water to heat its building and its brews. In the winter, the warm water running through closed pipes even helps keep the fermenting beer at the proper temperature.

All this gives Riff Raff the street cred as an "earth-powered brewery." It's housed in an 1896 Victorian-style house, one of the oldest in town, which only adds to the operation's unusual character. You can even rent rooms in the place on Airbnb, allowing for an easy crawl home at closing time.

The brewery makes six flagship beers, seasonals, and guest beers, all available in tasting flights to give you options. The **Skallywag English Pale Ale** is a throwback with sweet caramel malt as the dominant flavor rather than hops. The **Hopgoblin American IPA** is likewise traditional with the three C's of hops—cascade, centennial, and chinook.

On the food menu, the standout is the Walter burger, which features beer-brined smoked pulled pork.

STEAMWORKS BREWING COMPANY

801 E. Second Ave., Durango, CO 81301; (970) 259-9200; SteamworksBrewing.com
Founded: 1996 **Founders:** Kris Oyler and Brian McEachron **Brewer:** Ken Martin **Flagship beers:** Colorado Kölsch, Kenny's Pain Pils, Third Eye P.A., Steam Engine Lager, One Wit Wünder, Lizard Head Red, Weizenbock, Saison, Backside Stout **Seasonals/special releases:** Ale Diablo, Prescribed Burn, Golden Hefeweizen, Conductor, Quince Años Barleywine, Night Train, Imperial Mole Stout, Ale Sabor **Tours:** None **Taproom hours:** Mon through Wed, 11 a.m. to 11 p.m.; Thurs through Sat, 11 to 2 a.m.; Sun, 11 a.m. to midnight. Growlers and cans to go.

Steamworks opened in 1996 as the fourth Durango brewery in a town of just 2,000 people. Founders Kris Oyler and Brian McEachron set up their brewpub in a 1920s-era car dealership. Only a year after opening, Steamworks won a gold medal at GABF for its amber lager, **Steam Engine Lager**. In subsequent years, the beer went on to win even more accolades. Showing a knack for full-flavored and characterful lighter styles, the award-winning **Colorado Kölsch** followed. Now canned and distributed statewide, the two beers—along with the brewery's dry-hopped **Third Eye Pale Ale**—have

Beer Lover's Pick

COLORADO KÖLSCH

Style: Kölsch-Style Ale
ABV: 4.8 percent
Availability: Year-round on draft and in cans
The much-awarded Colorado Kölsch Ale is the first pour you should get at Steamworks Brewing. The Colorado flag–colored cans are available most places, and this is a great summit beer, but trying it from the source is just fresher. The light and crisp style offers a touch of hops and touch of fruitiness from the ale yeast. A blend of the best of all beer worlds, it's a great brew for any occasion.

gone on to successfully spread the Steamworks name far beyond its local southwestern reach. The servers are certified in beer knowledge, so rely on them for help in ordering from the lengthy brew list.

Much like a handful of other brewpubs in the state, Steamworks prides itself on sourcing the highest-quality ingredients for its lengthy, family-friendly menu. The appetizers include lettuce wraps and Cajun-dusted popcorn shrimp, and the main items include pizza, spicy southwestern dishes, and burgers. One of the special entrees is a full Cajun boil with Alaskan Dungeness crab, wild Texas shrimp, andouille sausage, new potatoes, and sweet corn.

THREE BARREL BREWING

475 Grand Ave., Del Norte, CO 81132; (719) 657-0681; ThreeBarrelBrew.com
Founded: 2005 **Founder:** John Bricker **Brewer:** John Bricker
Flagship beers: Trashy Blonde, Bad Phil, Hop Trash, Burnt Toast, Thursday Special **Seasonals/special releases:** Grammy Phil, Zigeunerweisen, Ol' Dairy Ale, Pumpelstiltskin, Pemba Sherpa, Chill Session, D Mountain Brown, Burros Wild, Goofy Foot, Freeze Cat, Scavezzo, Trippel Barrel, Threedom Wheat, Three Heavy, Keleto, Black Copter, Melaza, Chimayo, Morada, Saliente, Hermano, Tre Anasazz, Genizaro **Tours:** On request **Taproom hours:** Mon through Sun, 11 a.m. to 9 p.m. Growlers and bottles to go.

In what feels like the middle of nowhere, you'll find a brewery that generates attention one small batch at a time. Three Barrel Brewing is larger than it name suggests, but not by much. And neither is the town of Del Norte (pronounced "Del-nort" by the locals), whose population hovers near 1,500. The town along the Rio Grande sits at a junction east of Pagosa Springs and west of Alamosa, making it a pass-through for most. But Colorado beer fans know to stop at Three Barrel Brewing, which started in the back of founder and brewer John Bricker's insurance office but now resides next door to the business.

This is Coors territory in the San Luis Valley, where the mega Colorado brewer gets much of its grain. But Three Barrel specializes is esoteric sours in its Penitente Canyon series, so named for a canyon where a religious sect found solitude. The beers in the series are varying levels of funky, puckering, and complex, with some more balanced than others but all unique in part because of the mineral water in the area.

At the taproom, you can find more traditional styles, including a Belgian blonde, pale ale, IPA, brown ale, and coconut brown lager that remain on tap year-round. Pair one with a wood-fired pizza.

ALE HOUSE GRAND JUNCTION

2531 North 12th St., Grand Junction, CO 81501; (970) 242-7253; AleHouseGJ.com
Taps: 35

Started by Breckenridge Brewery and the Wynkoop Brewing team, this place is modeled off similar restaurants on the Front Range. Still, it gets one of the best selections of craft beer in the area, making it an good stop. The menu is divided into different categories, including "Gateway Craft Beers," "Craft Beer Connoisseur," and "You Are Not Worthy." As the descriptions suggest, there's something for everyone, and the place draws families and travelers alike.

The top-level craft beers include the likes of sours from Crooked Stave and Jolly Pumpkin and stouts from Fremont and New Holland. So it's not all just Breckenridge Brewery beers. The Colorado beer lineup includes nearby breweries that you may not have time to visit. So try Roaring Fork Beer Company and Palisade Brewing Company if you can find them on tap. Or reach across the border to try La Cumbre Brewing, a great brewery from neighboring New Mexico.

The food menu is better-than-average pub items with artichoke dip, shrimp tacos, Colorado bison burger, and teriyaki chicken satays, for example. The menu will offer pairings with beers, picked by the chef, and it changes seasonally. Hand-tossed pizzas are another menu option.

BEER FESTIVALS

beer festival is a great way to try a bunch of new breweries and beers all in one place or, better yet, test your palate and compare a single beer style from many brewers. In Colorado, there's a beer festival or two every weekend it seems, particularly in the summer. But not all festivals are the same, and too many feature redundant lists of breweries and big crowds more interested in quantity than quality. The best events break out of the mold, giving beer fans an opportunity to try unique brews and talk to the brewers behind the creations. The festivals listed in this chapter are the ones you should save a date on the calendar for each year and travel the state to visit.

January

BIG BEERS, BELGIANS & BARLEYWINES FESTIVAL

Beaver Run Resort and Conference Center, 620 Village Rd., Breckenridge, CO 80424; BigBeersFestival.com

ig Beers, Belgians and Barleywines Festival is one of the premier craft beer events in Colorado because it goes well beyond the traditional tasting session. The three-day event at a slopeside resort in Breckenridge offers special

beer dinners, educational seminars with elite brewers, a homebrew competition, and a tasting session featuring more than 400 beers. The education seminars—designed for beer geeks, homebrewers, and professionals—are what set Big Beers apart. The dinners pair top chefs and brewers in intimate gatherings. The commercial tasting features nearly 150 breweries pouring only beers that fit the name of the festival: Belgians, experimental brews, and those with ABV north of 7 percent. It's a heady festival given the mountain town's 9,600-foot elevation. The best way to experience the event is a weekend pass, but you can also buy tickets to individual events and attend side tap takeovers throughout town.

March

COLLABORATION FEST

Location varies, Denver, CO; CollaborationFest.com

ollaboration Fest is unlike most any beer festival you'll find. The event, cosponsored by the Colorado Brewers Guild, pairs the state's breweries with others from the same town or around the world to make unique one-off beers. And plenty of the industry's big names participate. The idea behind the festival is to celebrate the camaraderie at the center of the craft beer industry—even as it becomes a more competitive space—and let the brewers' imaginations run wild. The 100-plus beers often riff on traditional styles, combining elements from each brewery's home turf. But others go for an extreme twist, such as a

beer made with rocks or a dry-hopped malt liquor. The flavors will challenge your palate, and even if not all win the day, most will leave a mark on your beer imagination.

May

ODELL SMALL BATCH FESTIVAL

Odell Brewing Company, 800 E. Lincoln Ave., Fort Collins, CO 80524; OdellBrewing.com

Odell Small Batch Festival is an impressive show with 40-plus beers all from a single brewery. It started years ago as a free event where you bought tokens for beer, but it became too popular, and now it's a ticketed affair complete with live music, food trucks, and yard games. The ticket comes with a limited number of beers, but additional tokens for beers are available for purchase. The event shows how even veteran brewers continue to push the limits. And it is often a testing ground for new brews that the Fort Collins beer maker is refining behind the scenes. A version of Drumroll APA, a popular hazy pale ale, poured under a different iteration at Small Batch festival years ago. The rare offerings are limited and often draw long lines, so it's good to go early.

June

AVERY INVITATIONAL

Avery Brewing Company, 4910 Nautilus Ct. N, Boulder, CO 80301; AveryBrewing.com

Avery Brewing knows how to throw a party. The Boulder brewery's festivals rank among the best in the state. For years, Avery hosted separate events dedicated to different beer styles: IPAs, strong ales, and sours. More recently, the brewery consolidated them into a summer festival called the Avery Invitational, which featured a handpicked list of approximately 75 breweries selected by employees. The pour list reads like a who's who of the hottest breweries in the industry, and each poured some of the best beers you can find in the US. The format and timing of the festival, which takes place at the brewery, may change again in years to come. But whatever event Avery hosts, make sure to attend. ***Tip:*** Buy tickets early, as they always sell out.

BURNING CAN FESTIVAL

Bohn Park, 199 2nd Ave., Lyons, CO 80540; oskarblues.com/ event/burning-can-festival

It's hard to describe the Burning Can Festival in a small space, but it's easy to say it's unlike any other. Here's what you can expect: a beer run relay, whitewater kayak races, camping, and, of course, a giant burning can. The event hosted by Oskar Blues Brewery takes place each summer to coincide with the Lyons Outdoor games in the town where the brewer got its start. When it comes to the beer, the Saturday afternoon festival features more than 70 craft breweries and some 250 brews. Most of the breweries are from Colorado and neighboring states, but Oskar Blues showcases its portfolio of siblings with Cigar City, Perrin Brewing, and more attending the event. If you're up to the challenge, compete in a morning beer relay race where trail runners must drink a can before finishing each lap.

session are reserved for members of the American Homebrewers Association or Brewers Association, and it is the best session to attend because it is less crowded and rowdy. Outside the festival, check out the tap takeovers and special events that take place across the city and combine to represent the best celebration of beer in the US.

November

NITRO FEST

Roosevelt Park, 700 Longs Peak Ave., Longmont, CO 80501; LeftHandBrewing.com/nitro-fest

Left Hand Brewing's Nitro Fest is dedicated to the tiny cascading bubbles of nitrogen that make these special beers a dream to drink. The festival is the only one in the world that features exclusively nitrogenated beers, according to the brewery. It's a celebration of Left Hand's Nitro Milk Stout, which is a hallmark in the craft beer world. The uniqueness of the event is accentuated by the scene. The festival takes place in a large tent where circus acts, dancers, fire spinners, and costumed drinkers create a fantastical beer world. The breweries invited in years past included Dogfish Head, Firestone Walker, and New Holland, and the styles cover the board from light to dark, all on nitrogen.

December

DENVER BEER FESTIVUS

Location varies. Denver, CO; DenverBeerFestivus.com

The Denver Beer Festivus—so named for the Seinfeld-created holiday—features only the city's brewers. It's a familiar list of names and beers, but take a step back to appreciate what it represents: an opportunity to taste the vast scale of Denver's beer scene. The number of breweries in the city has exploded in recent years, and Festivus offers a place to try them all at once and toast what makes the scene so great. Not to mention that it's a holiday-themed festival, so wear grandma's hand-knit Santa sweater or flashing holiday light necklace—it's all for fun anyway.

BEER STORES

Colorado's rich beer culture extends to its family-owned liquor stores, many of which curate their brewery lists like a cicerone or sommelier. For decades, the state restricted liquor stores to a single location and only recently began to loosen the laws to allow for multiple locations and full-strength beer sales at grocery and convenience stores.

So even if it takes a little extra effort to find the best beers, the deep knowledge at these bottle shops in Colorado makes it worth the trip. It's also important to note that local liquor stores get different selections and often sell local breweries you can't find at grocery and convenience stores. Most bottle shops listed below update their social media accounts with the latest releases. *Tip:* Once you grab a few Colorado beers, give a look at others from the Rocky Mountain region and West Coast that you can't find in other states.

ARGONAUT WINE & LIQUORS

760 E. Colfax Ave., Denver, CO 80203; ArgonautLiquor.com; @ArgonautLiquor

The warehouse-sized liquor store in downtown Denver proudly declares, "Argonaut has it." And when it comes to the beer selection, the motto fits. Argonaut's size means it gets more beer than its smaller counterparts and takes longer to sell out of the good stuff.

On the opposite side of the aisle from the beer cooler, the top shelf features rare brews from around the country with quantities often subject to limits, such as California's Russian River sours and Colorado's **Copper Kettle** stouts. Farther toward the back, a cooler is dedicated to selling single bottles for mixed six-packs. The store opens at 8 a.m. every day, making it a convenient stop before heading out to the mountains or the airport.

ASPEN WINE & SPIRITS

300 Puppy Smith St., Aspen, CO 81611;
AspenWineAndSpirits.com

Tucked away from the main street on the north side of town, opposite the ski hill, Aspen Wine & Spirits is the go-to place for the best selection in the area. It's located next to a grocery store, and the shop accepts call-in orders and even offers free delivery service.

The beer to buy is the local Aspen Brewing Company, which distributes to only a handful of states. The brewery closed its downtown taproom but remains available on tap throughout town. Other local choices that don't always make it to all parts of the state include Roaring Fork Beer Company.

BASECAMP WINE & SPIRITS

223 Lusher Ct., Frisco, CO 80443; BaseCampLiquors.com;
Facebook.com/BaseCampLiquors

The reason to visit Basecamp Wine & Spirits is the bomber room—a walk-in cooler featuring 22-ounce bottles and other rare beers on head-to-toe shelves. There's so much beer, but it feels good to linger in the cold surrounded by bottled friends.

The store is located just off I-70 and across the parking lot from Outer Range Brewing Company, a convenient stop for anyone headed into the mountains or back to Denver. It offers a "pick 6 program" to let you build your own six-pack of beer as well as free in-store tastings Friday and Saturday evenings. Both are great ways to discover beers you've never tasted.

COOPER WINE & SPIRITS

732 Cooper Ave., Glenwood Springs, CO 81601; CooperWine
AndSpirits.com

Cooper touts more than 350 craft beers at its shop in downtown Glenwood Springs, just off I-70 in the western stretch of the state. How do they pick? Well, the owners say they create partnerships with brewers who reward them with exclusive offerings, which makes for a distinctive beer list.

One of those partnerships is with Casey Brewing and Blending, one of the state's best and hardest-to-find breweries. As the brewery's hometown shop, it gets the deepest inventory of Casey beers, including certain styles that don't make it to Denver, so it's a frequent stop for the state's most discerning beer drinkers.

CRAFT ALLEY

1455 S. Pearl St., Denver, CO; Denver.CraftAlley.co; @Craft_Alley

Craft Alley is dedicated to the almighty crowler. The 32-ounce cans (the size of a half growler) are perfect for sharing with others or the occasions when you want two pints because it's that good. And crowlers are all that Craft Alley sells.

The shop partners with a rotating list of Denver-area breweries to fill the crowlers fresh from the tap with beers you typically can't buy in cans or bottles. The website lists the breweries and the latest beers, or you can call the shop to check inventory. And the best part: You don't even need to visit. Craft Alley will deliver to you and offers a membership program that allows you to pick the beers you want.

HAZEL'S BEVERAGE WORLD

1955 28th St., Boulder, CO 80301; HazelsBoulder.com; @HazelsBoulder

Hazel's is not your typical college-town liquor store. It's so big that there's a plane hanging from the ceiling, along with a huge tasting bar, cellar room, humidor, and "beer hangar" cooler. The company's slogan is "Same planet—Different world," so the out-of-mind experience makes sense.

The Boulder store was founded by a University of Colorado alumnus and a Colorado native. It boasts more than 2,700 different beers, and more than half of them are craft offerings, making it the largest selection in the area. The shop also has its own "frequent-flyer" program, in which it awards "miles" for purchases that can be redeemed for discounts and merchandise. Look for local breweries that only distribute, such as Acidulous Brewing Company.

MOLLY'S SPIRITS

5809 W. 44th Ave., Denver, CO 80212; MollysSpirits.com; @
MollysSpirits

Molly's Spirits looks like a museum for booze. And it takes a tour to get a look at all the displays, shelves, and stacks of cases. But the massive red "beer" sign on the back wall is a good place to start scanning the 65-plus cooler doors and a walk-in bomber room.

Just so you can take your time, the dozen-plus television screens throughout the store will keep you updated on the score of the game. To get the best beers, become a member of the beer club, and they'll let you know when the special releases debut. Also look for exclusive collaborations with New Image Brewing Company and others.

MONDO VINO

3601 W. 32nd Ave., Denver, CO 80211; MondoVinoDenver
.com; Facebook.com/MondoVinoDenver

Mondo Vino is the best of both worlds—an elite bottle shop and corner liquor store in one package. Located on the corner of Highlands Square, its friendly customer service is what sets the shop apart. It's the kind of place where the beer buyer knows his frequent customers, and even if you're new, he can help you find the beer for any mood.

The beer cooler consumes an entire wall and more, beckoning from the top of two stairs above the wooden wine racks and liquor shelves. It's a carefully curated selection with the best Colorado beers and rare bottles from other top breweries across the country.

MR. B'S WINE & SPIRITS

2101 Market St., #112, Denver, CO 80205;
MrBsWineAndSpirits.com; Facebook.com/
MrBsWineAndSpirits

Located in the Ballpark neighborhood, Mr. B's Wine & Spirits is the best beer store you can find close to the light rail and downtown hotels. It offers 500 different beers with a particular emphasis on best-in-class offerings from across the world.

The shop often gets Colorado breweries you can't find elsewhere, including Casey Brewing, and is rewarded by fans with best bottle shop awards. Also look for Larimer Beer, a local brewery that doesn't have a taproom yet. Make sure to check the cold case for the fresh beers and the shelves for the ones you can cellar for a few years.

SMALL BATCH LIQUORS

4340 Tennyson St., Denver, CO 80212; SmallBatchLiquors .com; Facebook.com/SmallBatchLiquors

Small Batch Liquors is just as the name suggests. It's tucked in a small house set back from the bustling Tennyson Street in Denver's Berkeley neighborhood. Shopping here is like an Easter egg hunt for the best brews. Look for breweries that don't have taprooms, such as Denver's Amalgam Brewing, whose taproom is only open sporadically.

Most thirsty patrons will focus first on the bottles but take a moment to appreciate the handcrafted wooden shelves, which rise from the floor to the ceiling and flow through the store like well-poured beer. The small space makes for an intimate occasion, so don't be shy and ask for help. Often, there's a special beer hiding on the shelves that you won't want to miss.

WILBUR'S TOTAL BEVERAGE

2201 S. College Ave., Fort Collins, CO 80525; WilbursTotalBeverage.com; Facebook.com/WilbursTotalBev

If you're sitting at a bar or brewery in beer-soaked Fort Collins and ask for a good place to buy beer, the bartenders will probably send you to Wilbur's. It is the big player in town with 25,000 square feet of liquor, wine, and beer spread across enough shelves that it feels like an adult maze.

The employees are great guides, thankfully. And because you're in Fort Collins, be sure to try the local breweries you couldn't fit into the tour. The beer tastings on Friday afternoons are a great excuse to make a stop, too.

WYATT'S WET GOODS

1250 Hover St., Longmont, CO 80501; WyattsWetGoods.com; Facebook.com/WyattsWetGoods

The name of Longmont's largest liquor store is unmistakable. And Wyatt's Wet Goods, a private family-owned business, specializes in craft beer. The store posts a huge selection and offers special deals on Colorado beers and American craft breweries each month. It's located next to a grocery store, making it a convenient stop for provisions and wet goods. The local breweries on the shelves include Wibby and Oskar Blues, and the knowledgeable staff can help you find anything else you need.

BYOB
Brew Your Own Beer

IF YOU WANT TO KNOW HOW HARD IT IS TO BREW GREAT BEER, TRY IT YOURSELF. COLORADO'S TOP BREWERIES GENEROUSLY SHARED A DOZEN RECIPES FOR THEIR COMMERCIAL BEERS TO ALLOW HOMEBREWERS TO MAKE A CLONE VERSION. MOST OF THE FOLLOWING RECIPES HAVE BEEN SCALED TO YIELD FIVE GALLONS OF BEER WHEN FINISHED. IF YOU HAVE QUESTIONS OR NEED CONVERSIONS TO EXTRACT BEER RECIPES, CONSULT WITH YOUR LOCAL HOMEBREW SHOP.

Beer Recipes

AVERY WHITE RASCAL

The easy-drinking, have-another Belgian-style witbier is the Avery Brewing's most popular. The unfiltered beer features coriander and orange peel to give it a little burst of flavor on an otherwise clean malt bill.

OG: 1.050; FG: 1.010; IBU: 23; SRM: 3; ABV: 5.6 percent

Malt:

> *5 pounds pale 2-Row*
> *5 pounds white wheat*

Hops:

> *0.15 ounce Bravo 15.6 percent AA (60 minutes)*
> *0.2 ounce Bravo 15.6 percent AA (30 minutes)*
> *0.27 ounce Sterling 6.8 percent AA (0 minutes)*
> *0.18 ounce Hersbrucker 4.5 percent AA (0 minutes)*

Spices:

> *0.31 ounce Coriander (0 minutes)*
> *0.07 ounce Bitter Orange Peel (0 minutes)*
> *0.28 ounce Sweet Orange Peel (0 minutes)*

Yeast:

> *Belgian Witbier Yeast (Wyeast 3944)*

Mash at 152°F and mash out at 165°F. Boil for 60 minutes, following hop schedule. Add the spice at flame out. Ferment at 66°F for 75 percent of the fermentation and raise the temperature to 77°F for diacetyl rest.

COURTESY OF AVERY BREWING COMPANY

BANDED OAK DRUNKARD'S CLOAK AMERICAN STRONG ALE

Banded Oak Brewing in Denver specializes in wine barrel–aged beers. Their 2018 GABF medal winner Drunkard's Cloak is a strong ale with vanilla beans that is typically aged in pinot noir barrels. Even without the wine barrels, this recipe makes a robust beer with deep malt flavors, and it will keep you as warm as a cloak.

OG: 1.083; FG: 1.018; IBU: 22; SRM: 14.9; ABV: 9.2 percent

Malt:

12 pounds 2-row

0.6 pound brown

0.3 pound crystal 120

0.5 pound flaked wheat

0.2 pound chocolate

0.03 pound roasted barley

Hops:

0.5 ounce Centennial 10 percent AA (75 minutes)

0.1 ounce Golding (0 minutes)

Adjuncts:

1 pound cane sugar

0.03 pound lactose sugar

2 vanilla beans

Yeast:

American Ale (Wyeast 1056)

A single mash infusion at 158°F with a 60-minute rest and recirculation until clear. Batch sparge until 7 gallons is collected. Boil for 75 minutes following the hop schedule. Add cane and lactose sugar in the final 15 minutes. Ferment at 68°F. Once primary fermentation is complete, transfer to secondary and add vanilla beans (sliced down the center and chopped to expose the bean). Cool to 32°F before bottling or kegging.

COURTESY OF BANDED OAK BREWING COMPANY

CALL TO ARMS
MORE LIKE BORE-O-PHYLL

This IPA took home a gold medal at the 2018 World Beer Cup Championships. The beer is packed with strong notes of orange zest, ripe peach, and spruce tips thank to the whole-cone hops used at the brewery.

OG: 1.059; FG: 1.008; IBU: 63; SRM: 4.6; ABV: 6.7 percent

Malt:

10 pounds American 2-row
1 pound Weyermann rye
0.75 pound Weyermann Munich II
0.25 pound acidulated
0.5 pound flaked oats

Hops:

0.5 ounce Centennial 8.1 percent AA (10 minutes)
0.4 ounce Waimea 18 percent AA (10 minutes)
0.75 ounce Galaxy 17.4 percent AA (0 minutes)
0.5 ounce Citra 12.8 percent AA (0 minutes)
0.5 ounce Waimea 18 percent AA (0 minutes)
0.25 ounce Centennial 8.1 percent AA (0 minutes)
24 ounces of Cascade fresh hops or whole cone (0 minutes)
0.66 ounce Amarillo (dry hop)
0.33 ounce Galaxy (dry hop)
0.66 ounce Mosaic (dry hop)

Yeast:

American Ale Yeast (Wyeast 1056)

A single-infusion mash at standard temperatures. Boil for 60 minutes, following hop schedule. Ferment at standard temperatures for the yeast and add dry hops according to schedule.

COURTESY OF CALL TO ARMS BREWING COMPANY

DRY DOCK APRICOT BLONDE

Dry Dock's original location is attached to the Brew Hut, the homebrew store that started it all. And there you can buy the ingredients to make the brewery's flagship beer, Apricot Blonde, while drinking an Apricot Blonde.

OG: 1.047–1.051; FG: 1.011–1.015; IBU: 15–19; ABV: 4.7 percent

Malt:

> *9.5 pounds 2-row*
> *0.375 pound English medium crystal*

Hops:

> *0.75 ounce Cascade (60 minutes)*

Yeast:

> *Dry Ale Yeast (Safale S-04)*

Additions:

> *1–4 ounces apricot flavoring (to taste)*

Mash the grains at 152°F for 60 minutes. Boil the wort for 60 minutes, adding the hops at the start. Ferment at 60°F to 68°F with the option of transferring to a secondary fermentation for the final days. Stir in the apricot flavoring to taste before bottling or kegging.

COURTESY OF DRY DOCK BREWING COMPANY

BYOB

FUNKWERKS SAISON

Saison (French for "season") is the name given to pale ales brewed seasonally in farmhouses in the French-speaking region of Belgium. These ales were made for the farmworkers during harvest season. Funkwerks Saison is a celebration of the modern saison style with citrus and pepper tastes and a dry finish.

OG: 1.056; FG: 1.005; IBU: 25; SRM: 5; ABV: 6.5 percent

Malt:

4.7 pounds Pilsner

3.6 pounds 2-row

1.1 pounds Munich

1 pound pale wheat

Hops:

0.75 ounce Opal (60 minutes)

0.5 ounce Opal (15 minutes)

1 ounce Opal (flame out)

0.5 ounce Opal (dry-hop, 7 days)

Yeast:

French Saison (Wyeast 3711)

Mash at 152°F for 60 minutes. Boil for 60 minutes. Pitch yeast at 68°F and allow the temperature to free rise to 73°F. Hold at this temperature until fermentation is complete, then dry-hop with 0.5 ounce of Opal for 7 days.

COURTESY OF FUNKWERKS

GRIMM BROTHERS SNOW DROP

When the *Reinheitsgebot* declared that German beer was pure only if it consisted solely of water, barley, hops, and yeast, kottbusser ale became all but extinct, as it contains oats, molasses, and honey. Snow Drop is Grimm Brothers' homage to resurrect the style.

OG: 1.054; FG: 1.013; IBU: 16; SRM: 4; ABV: 7

Malt:

6 pounds pilsen

3.8 pounds wheat

0.7 pound flaked oats

Hops:

0.05 ounce Hallertau (first wort hop)

0.25 ounce Magnum (75 minutes)

0.25 ounce Hallertau (30 minutes)

0.5 ounce Hallertau (0 minutes)

1 ounce Saaz (0 minutes)

Adjuncts:

0.6 ounce molasses

1.3 ounce honey

Yeast:

German Ale/Kölsch Yeast (White Labs WLP029)

Mash at 152°F for 60 minutes and sparge at 168°F. Boil for 90 minutes, following the hop schedule and adding the molasses and honey in the last 5 minutes of the boil. Ferment at 63°F until complete.

COURTESY OF GRIMM BROTHERS BREWHOUSE

PAGOSA POOR RICHARD'S ALE

Poor Richard's Ale is an all-American, colonial-style ale brewed to commemorate Ben Franklin's 300th birthday. This modern-day interpretation of the colonists' brown ale is brewed with corn and spiced with molasses, a common sweetener back then.

OG: 1.068; FG: 1.018; IBU: 27; SRM: 17; ABV 6.8 percent

Malt:

7.4 pounds pale

2.4 pounds flaked corn

1.6 pounds biscuit

0.875 pound special roast

0.13 pound black patent

Hops:

0.7 ounce Kent Goldings (60 minutes)

0.7 ounce Kent Goldings (45 minutes)

0.7 ounce Kent Goldings (30 minutes)

Adjuncts:

3 ounces molasses

Yeast:

English Ale Yeast (White Labs WLP002 or Wyeast 1968) or Scottish Ale Yeast (White Labs WLP028 or Wyeast 1728)

Mash at 154°F for at least 45 minutes or until conversion is complete. Boil for 90 minutes, adding the molasses in the last 15 minutes of the boil. Ferment at 68°F until complete.

COURTESY PAGOSA BREWING COMPANY

POST SUMMER TEATH

Post Brewing's Summer Teath is an American IPA with an infusion of green tea. It makes for a light, refreshing IPA in the summer months with a result similar to sipping an iced tea. The brewery uses tea from Pekoe Sip House in Boulder, but other brands will do.

OG: 1.036; FG: 1.009; IBU: 55; ABV: 4.1

Malt:

> *3.5 pounds 2-row*
> *2.625 pounds red wheat*
> *0.25 pound acidulated*
> *0.3 pound crystal 15L*

Hops:

> *0.25 ounce CTZ 17.9 percent AA (60 minutes)*
> *0.15 ounce Pekko 15.5 percent AA (30 minutes)*
> *0.7 ounce Azacca 12.8 percent AA (10 minutes)*
> *1.4 ounces Pekko 15.5 percent AA (0 minutes)*
> *1.7 ounces Azacca 12.8 percent AA (0 minutes)*
> *1.3 ounces Pekko (dry hop)*
> *1.3 ounces Azacca (dry hop)*

Tea:

> *1.8 ounces green tea in a mesh bag (10 minutes)*

Yeast:

> *California Ale Yeast (White Labs WLP001)*

Mash grains for 60 minutes at 149°F at a liquor-to-grist ratio of 2.85 to 1. Boil for 65 minutes, following the hop schedule and adding tea for final 10 minutes of boil. Ferment at 65°F until gravity hits 1.018 and then raise temperature to 72°F until final gravity is reached. Cold condition for 7 days at 32°F.

COURTESY OF POST BREWING COMPANY

SEEDSTOCK BOHEMIAN ALE

Seedstock Brewery in Denver makes a hoppy amber beer that is malty and crisp. It uses the unique Czech Kazbek hop, which is a hybrid of the traditional Czech Saaz. Kazbek has many of the Saaz characteristics, such as an earthy, peppery spiciness as well as a unique fruity and lemon aroma.

OG: 1.061; FG: 1.011; IBU: 56; SRM: 12.7; ABV: 6.6 percent

Malt:

> 9 pounds Bohemian pilsner
> 1.3 pounds Vienna
> 0.75 pound caraaroma
> 0.75 pound carafoam
> 0.2 pound rice hulls

Hops:

> 1.2 ounces Kazbek (90 minutes)
> 1 ounce Perle (90 minutes)
> 1.2 ounces Kazbek (15 minutes)
> 1 ounce Perle (15 minutes)
> 0.5 ounce Kazbek (0 minutes)
> 0.5 ounce Perle (0 minutes)

Yeast:

> Golden Kölsch Style Ale Yeast (Inland Island INIS-572)

Mash at 148°F for 60 minutes. Boil for 90 minutes, following the hop schedule. Ferment at 60°F.

COURTESY OF SEEDSTOCK BREWERY

STEAMWORKS STEAM ENGINE LAGER

Refreshing, clean, and malty, Steam Engine Lager is beautiful, clear, and amber in color. Another super-versatile brew, this recipe has won awards at many festivals, including the GABF and World Beer Cup.

OG: 1.050; FG: 1.010; IBU: 22; SRM: 11

Malt:

> 6.7 pounds pale
>
> 0.75 pound crystal 15L
>
> 0.75 pound crystal 60L
>
> 0.75 pound light Munich
>
> 0.375 pound crystal 75L

Hops:

> 0.4 ounce Chinook (90 minutes)
>
> 0.2 ounce Cascade (30 minutes)
>
> 1 ounce Cascade (0 minutes)

Yeast:

> California Lager (Wyeast 2112)

Mash at 152°F for 60 minutes. Boil for 90 minutes. Ferment at 59°F until 75 percent attenuated and then let the beer rise to 64°F for a diacetyl rest.

COURTESY OF STEAMWORKS BREWING COMPANY

WELDWERKS JUICY BITS NEW ENGLAND–STYLE IPA

WeldWerks Juicy Bits is one of the best hazy IPAs in America. The beer, as the name suggests, tastes like tropical fruit juice thanks to the big hop additions, soft mouthfeel, and subtle bitterness. It take a lot of hops to make this beer, so beware. But your taste buds will thank you for it.

OG: 1.066; FG: 1.015; IBU: 55; ABV: 6.7 percent

Malt:

> *10 pounds pale*
> *1 pound flaked wheat*
> *1 pound flaked oats*
> *0.75 pound dextrin*

Hops:

> *0.15 ounce Mosaic 13.1 percent AA (first wort hop)*
> *0.15 ounce Citra 12.5 percent AA (first wort hop)*
> *0.15 ounce El Dorado 14.8 percent AA (first wort hop)*
> *0.2 ounce Mosaic 13.1 percent AA (40 minutes whirlpool)*
> *0.2 ounce Citra 12.5 percent AA (40 minutes whirlpool)*
> *0.2 ounce El Dorado 14.8 percent AA (40 minutes whirlpool)*
> *0.45 ounce Mosaic 13.1 percent AA (30 minutes whirlpool)*
> *0.45 ounce Citra 12.5 percent AA (30 minutes whirlpool)*
> *0.45 ounce El Dorado 14.8 percent AA (30 minutes whirlpool)*
> *0.6 ounce Mosaic 13.1 percent AA at 20 minutes (when whirlpool is shut off)*
> *0.6 ounce Citra 12.5 percent AA at 20 minutes (when whirlpool is shut off)*
> *0.6 ounce El Dorado 14.8 percent AA at 20 minutes (when whirlpool is shut off)*
> *0.65 ounce Mosaic 13.1 percent AA (dry-hop for 8 days once gravity reaches 1.020–1.022)*
> *0.65 ounce Citra 12.5 percent AA (dry-hop for 8 days once gravity reaches 1.020–1.022)*
> *0.65 ounce El Dorado 14.8 percent AA (dry-hop for 8 days once gravity reaches 1.020–1.022)*
> *1 ounce Mosaic 13.1 percent AA (dry-hop for 4 days)*
> *1 ounce Citra 12.5 percent AA (dry-hop for 4 days)*
> *1 ounce El Dorado 14.8 percent AA (dry-hop for 4 days)*

Yeast:

London Ale III Yeast (Wyeast 1318)

Water:

Use calcium chloride and calcium sulfate additions to adjust water profile to about 175–200 ppm chloride, 75–100 ppm sulfate, and 125–150 ppm calcium.

Mash at 149°F for 60 minutes or until conversion is complete. Add half of the calcium chloride and calcium sulfate additions to the mash and the rest at sparge. Add the first wort hops during runoff, immediately after vorlauf, and allow them to steep in the hot wort as the mash is sparged.

Boil for 60 minutes. Once complete, whirlpool for 40 minutes, following the hop schedule.

Pitch the yeast and ferment at 67°F for 2 to 3 days, then allow the temperature to rise slowly to 73°F by the end of fermentation to ensure full attenuation. When fermentation reaches 1.020 to 1.022 gravity, add the first dry-hop addition. About 4 days later, add the second dry-hop addition for another 4 days.

COURTESY OF WELDWERKS BREWING COMPANY

WIT'S END SLAM DUNKELWEIZEN

This is an old favorite from Wit's End Brewing in Denver, which paired with Strange Craft Beer Company to create a dynamic duo. Slam Dunkelweizen combines roasted wheat with Hefeweizen yeast strains, creating a taste that mimics chocolate-chip banana bread. The Dunkelweizen style works well in any season because of its light body, fruity notes, and sweet, roasted base.

OG: 1.055; FG: 1.012; IBU: 15; SRM: 22; ABV: 5.6 percent

Malt:

4 pounds white wheat

2.6 pounds Pilsner

14 ounces honey

7 ounces Cara-Pils/Dextrine

6.1 ounces Munich

4.7 ounces rye

4.7 ounces biscuit

4.7 ounces Special B

4.7 ounces crystal 70-80L

4.7 ounces caramel wheat

4.7 ounces chocolate wheat

Hops:

0.15 ounce Columbus (60 minutes)

0.5 ounce Tettnang (30 minutes)

0.2 ounce Tettnang (15 minutes)

Yeast:

Hefeweizen Ale Yeast (Wyeast 3068 or White Labs 300)

Mash at 151°F for 75 minutes and sparge at 170°F. Boil for 75 minutes. Pitch 1 package of yeast (a starter is not recommended) and ferment between 72°F and 75°F for 5 to 7 days or until complete. A secondary at cellar temperature for 2 weeks is recommended.

COURTESY OF WIT'S END BREWING COMPANY

In the Kitchen

For years, wine found a place into the cook's repertoire—but not as much beer. Now that's beginning to change, and more recipes are incorporating beer as an ingredient in dishes, not to mention as a complement to a meal. Depending on the style of beer added to a recipe, the flavors can vary from sweet, fruity, or bitter to notes of chocolate or coffee. And beer also is a great base for a creative cocktail. This chapter offers recipes for sauces, appetizers, entrees, desserts, and beer cocktails that you can make at home.

STONEHENGE STOUT BARBECUE SAUCE

Bull & Bush brewpub's barbecue sauce recipe is just simple and interesting enough to make it stand out. A stout serves as the base for the recipe.

¼ cup apple cider

½ teaspoon tabasco

½ tablespoon liquid smoke

⅓ cup brown sugar

1 pint (16 ounces) Stonehenge Stout beer

1½ tablespoons granulated garlic

1½ tablespoons celery seeds

1 cup Worcestershire sauce

¼ cup molasses

¼ cup chile powder

4 cups ketchup

Heat all ingredients on stove and let simmer for 20 minutes. Cool and enjoy.

COURTESY OF BULL & BUSH PUB & BREWERY

BLACKBERRY SAISON GLAZE

Tart meets funk in this far-from-boring blackberry glaze. Freshcraft suggests using the glaze on fish, but it can also double as a delicious salad dressing.

½ cup yellow onion

2 teaspoons minced garlic

1 pint blackberries, washed

½ cup sherry vinegar

1 cup water

1 cup white sugar

½ cup Funkwerks Saison at room temperature

Place all ingredients except the saison into a saucepan, adding the sugar last to prevent burning.

Bring the mixture to a boil, then reduce to a simmer. When the mixture reaches 235°F, remove from the heat and whisk in the saison. Allow the glaze to cool before serving.

Freshcraft uses this glaze on Mahi Mahi served with cornbread and jalapeño corn sauté.

COURTESY OF FRESHCRAFT

HABANERO FIG JAM

Thirsty Monk Brewing in Denver uses its stout as the base to create a delectable fig jam that is a great accompaniment to cheese and charcuterie or on a fresh baguette.

1 teaspoon sunflower oil (canola is an acceptable substitute)
¼ cup yellow onion, minced
1 habanero, seeded and minced
1 ¼ pounds dried figs, cut in half and stems removed
3 ounces molasses
3 ounces cider vinegar
2 tablespoons lime juice
12 ounces Thirsty Monk Brewery Brother Noah Stout
1 ½ teaspoons salt

Heat the oil in a medium saucepan, add onions and habanero, and sweat until translucent. Add the figs and molasses and stir to coat. Add remaining liquids and salt. Allow to simmer until approximately one-half of the liquid has reduced or been absorbed by the figs. Puree to desired consistency.

COURTESY OF THIRSTY MONK BREWING

HOWDY CHEESE SOUP

Post Brewing uses its Howdy Western Pilsner to make this cheese soup, which is a popular pub dish to pair with beer.

½ pound unsalted butter

1 cup yellow onion, finely diced

1 cup flour

1¾ cups Post Howdy Western Pilsner

¾ pound of cream cheese, cut into smaller chunks

2 quarts milk (vitamin D or 2 percent)

1 bay leaf

2 quarts cheddar cheese, grated

Salt and pepper to taste

Melt the butter in a pan over low to medium heat without letting the butter brown. As soon as the butter is melted, add the onions and cook on low to medium heat until the onions soften, again without browning. Once the onions are soft, about 5 to 7 minutes, slowly whisk in the flour to make a roux. Cook the roux mixture on low to medium heat for 5 minutes, stirring or whisking constantly.

Whisk in the Howdy Western Pilsner, being careful not to splatter. Once the Howdy is whisked in well, bring it to a soft simmer. Be careful not to let it boil, or the pilsner will turn bitter and the soup will be ruined. Whisk or stir frequently as the soup begins to thicken. Be careful to not let the bottom burn, as the soup will start to stick to the bottom if allowed. Once the beer and roux mixture has simmered and thickened, add the cream cheese in small chunks until it's fully melted. Next, add the milk and bay leaf and bring to a light simmer again. Remember not to let it boil.

Simmer the soup until the mix starts to thicken again and then add the cheddar cheese until it melts, stirring frequently. Give it a taste and season with salt and pepper. Serve in warm bowls with some soft, crusty bread.

COURTESY OF POST BREWING

BEER-CRUSTED CHEESE DIPPERS

A gourmet twist on mozzarella sticks, these cheese dippers up the ante on everyday appetizers. The process may be a bit time consuming, but the results are well worth the effort.

1 cup cornstarch
2 cups pale ale (Odell Brewing Company 5 Barrel Pale Ale)
4 medium eggs
1 box cheese crackers
2 cups panko
4 cups of your favorite melting cheese in ¾-inch cubes

Whisk together the cornstarch, ale, and eggs. Add the cheese crackers and the panko to a food processor and fully combine. Divide the cheese into four portions. Use your hands to mix each cheese portion individually into the slurry of ale, then strain lightly. Add this to the cracker mixture in a large bowl. Repeat this process two more times for each cheese portion. In the end, this should be a total of 3 "breadings" per portion. Let sit for at least an hour before frying at 350°F.

Freshcraft serves the cheese dippers topped with crumbled gorgonzola and house-made smoked onion ketchup and cashew-spinach pesto for dipping.

COURTESY OF FRESHCRAFT

PBR BANGS ISLAND MUSSELS

Euclid Hall's mussels are made with Pabst Blue Ribbon, but a light American lager from a local brewery also will do the trick. The same beer style is what pairs best with this dish.

12 ounces Bangs Island mussels, cleaned
1 teaspoon garlic, minced
1 tablespoon shallots, minced
4 ounces Pabst Blue Ribbon Beer
4 ounces vegetable stock
1 tablespoon basil chiffonade
1 teaspoon thyme, chopped
2 ounces cold butter
2 teaspoons lemon juice
Grilled sourdough

In a hot sauté pan, add mussels, garlic, and shallots. Sauté until garlic is just starting to turn golden, deglaze with beer, bring to a boil, add stock, and cover. Once mussels have opened, remove lid and finish with herbs and butter. Season and serve in a large bowl with lemon juice on the side. Top with grilled sourdough.

COURTESY OF EUCLID HALL BAR & KITCHEN

BÓ KHO

A take on the traditional dish Bó Kho, this recipe uses Great Divide Brewing's Hercules Double IPA. It is the creation of Ryan Gorby, the executive chef at Cho77, the sister restaurant to ChoLon.

2 pounds of beef chuck or stewing meat cut into 1.5-inch cubes

2 tablespoons ginger, peeled and minced

1 tablespoon curry powder

2 tablespoons brown or palm sugar

¼ cup fish sauce

2 garlic cloves, minced

1 yellow onion (medium-sized), diced

1 tablespoon paprika

4 star anise, whole

1 cinnamon stick

1 stalk lemongrass, cut into thirds and bruised

¾ pound carrot, peeled and cut into 1-inch segments

2 cups canned tomato, crushed

1½ cups beef broth

1 teaspoon salt

1 bottle Great Divide Hercules Double IPA

Mix beef with the ginger, curry powder, sugar, and fish sauce and allow to marinate for at least 30 minutes. In a medium-sized pot, heat the oil gently over low-medium heat.

Next, add the garlic, onions, and paprika and sweat lightly for about 2 minutes. Add the whole star anise, cinnamon stick, and bruised lemongrass pieces to cook for another 2 minutes.

Next, add the marinated beef and cook while stirring for about 5 minutes. After the beef is cooked, add the carrots, tomato, broth, salt, and beer to cover the beef.

Bring to a light simmer and cook uncovered until the beef is tender. When you are ready to serve, remove the lemongrass, cinnamon stick, and star anise pieces to avoid any surprises while eating.

Serve with shaved red onion, scallions, and beer-pickled garlic (see recipe on next page) over rice or with slices of fresh baguette. (**Note:** 2 teaspoons of Chinese five spice powder can be used in place of the star anise and cinnamon stick, but it should be added to the pot when the beef is added.)

COURTESY OF GREAT DIVIDE BREWING

BEER-PICKLED GARLIC

Another creation from Ryan Gorby, the pickled garlic goes nicely in the Bó Kho dish.

1 cup rice vinegar

½ cup sugar

½ cup Great Divide Hercules Double IPA

¼ cup water

1 teaspoon salt

8 cloves of garlic, sliced thin

Combine all the ingredients, except for the garlic, in a small pot and gently heat while stirring. Heat just until all the sugar and salt have been dissolved, cool the liquid to room temperature, and pour over the sliced garlic. Allow the garlic to pickle for at least 8 hours before using.

COURTESY OF GREAT DIVIDE BREWING

HOPS & PIE IPA MAC & CHEESE

The Hops & Pie IPA Mac & Cheese is a standout. Hops & Pie spices this recipe to a perfection achieved only through years of working to find the utopian ratio of cream to pepper to fennel.

> 3 cups cream
> 1 teaspoon fennel seeds, whole
> 1 teaspoon coriander seeds, whole
> 1 teaspoon black peppercorns, whole
> 2 each fresh bay leaves
> 1 cup sharp cheddar, shredded
> Cracked black pepper (to taste)
> Tapatio (to taste)
> 3 cups elbow macaroni, cooked
> 1 cup peas, cooked
> ¼ cup braised smoked ham hock, shredded
> ¼ cup a West Coast–style IPA
> Salt and pepper (to taste)
> 1 tablespoon bacon, chopped
> ¼ cup bread crumbs

In a saucepan, add cream, fennel seeds, coriander seeds, peppercorns, and bay leaves. Turn heat up to high and bring to a boil. Once a boil is reached, reduce heat to medium and stir constantly to prevent burning.

Once cream is reduced, strain through a fine-mesh strainer into another saucepan. Return pan with strained cream to a medium flame and stir in the sharp cheddar. Add cracked black pepper and tapatio to taste.

Add macaroni, peas, and ham hock to the pan and stir well. Add IPA and continue stirring until hot. Add salt and pepper to taste and place in a large ramekin. Top with chopped bacon and bread crumbs. Bake in oven at 400°F until bread crumbs become golden brown and crispy.

COURTESY OF HOPS & PIE

CHOCOLATE BREAD PUDDING WITH LEFT HAND MILK STOUT NITRO WHIPPED CREAM

This recipe from chefs Tim Payne and Melissa Newell uses Left Hand Milk Stout Nitro to add more decadence to dessert.

The cake:

1 pound loaf French or Italian bread, cubed

3 cups milk

¼ cup heavy cream

½ cup Left Hand Milk Stout Nitro

1 cup sugar

1 cup packed light brown sugar

¼ cup cocoa powder

1 tablespoon vanilla extract

2 teaspoons almond extract

1½ teaspoons cinnamon

6 eggs, lightly beaten

8 ounces semisweet chocolate, grated

The whipped cream:

2 cups heavy cream

¼ cup sugar

¼ cup Left Hand Milk Stout Nitro

To make the cake, preheat oven to 325°F. Lightly grease a 13- by 9-inch baking dish and place the bread in the dish. In a large bowl, whisk together the milk, cream, and stout. Using another bowl, combine the sugar, brown sugar, and cocoa powder and mix well. Add the sugar mixture to the milk mixture and mix well.

Add the vanilla and almond extract and the cinnamon to the beaten eggs. Combine the egg mixture to the milk mixture and mix well. Stir the grated chocolate into the mixture. Pour the mixture over the cubed bread in the pan. Let the mixture stand, stirring occasionally for approximately 20 minutes or until the bread absorbs most of the milk mixture.

Bake pudding for 1 hour or until set. Check pudding by inserting a knife through the middle, and it should come out clean.

To make the whipped cream, use a whisk and whip the cream until slightly thick. Add the sugar and stout and whip until peaks form.

COURTESY OF LEFT HAND BREWING COMPANY

In the Kitchen

VANILLA PORTER BEERAMISU

Breckenridge Brewery's recipe elevates beer in this dessert to the status of deserving a special name: Beeramisu.

1 cup heavy whipping cream
8 ounces mascarpone cheese—Italian cream cheese
1 cup powdered sugar
1 tablespoon vanilla
2 eggs
48 lady finger cookies
12 ounces Breckenridge Vanilla Porter
½ cup cocoa powder

Whip heavy cream to soft peaks and set aside. Combine mascarpone, sugar, vanilla, and eggs by whipping them together. Fold the whipped cream into the cheese mixture. Quickly dip the lady fingers (one at a time) into the vanilla porter. Place these in a glass 8- by 8-inch casserole dish, making a single layer of dipped cookies. Cover the cookies with the cheese and cream mixture (½ inch thick). Dust with cocoa powder and repeat the process. Finish with dusted cocoa. Refrigerate for at least 2 hours before serving.

COURTESY OF BRECKENRIDGE BREWERY

Beer Cocktails

EUCLIDIAN 75 COCKTAIL

This concoction is a controlled explosion of bitter, sweet, and sour on your tongue, thanks to Euclid Hall. Mix it and let the fireworks fly.

1.5 ounces Leopold Bros. Gin

0.5 ounce fresh lemon juice

0.5 ounce simple syrup

7 ounces of Crabtree Berliner Weisse

Mix together the gin, lemon juice, and syrup. Top with Berliner Weisse.

COURTESY OF EUCLID HALL BAR & KITCHEN

RUSTY BUS COCKTAIL

A thicker variation of a Belgian Sunset cocktail, the Rusty Bus mixes chocolate with cherry into a malty sweet, brown-ale dream. A dangerous concoction, this drinkable dessert cocktail is best enjoyed in slow sips.

1 ounce Van Gogh Dutch Chocolate Vodka

½ ounce Luxardo Cherry Liqueur

8½ ounces Avery Ellie's Brown Ale

Add vodka and cherry liqueur in a glass. Top off with ale.

COURTESY OF THE WEST END TAVERN

Pub Crawls

The dense concentration of breweries and bars in Colorado's main beer hubs makes it easy to put together daylong tours. In Denver alone, there are a handful of neighborhoods with enough beer spots to keep you entertained. This section represents the best ones and include breweries not mentioned elsewhere in the book because there's no shortage of great beer in Colorado.

Outside Denver, the best places for a beer tour are Fort Collins, where you can bike between pints, and Boulder, which requires a little extra travel to hit the best spots. Not included in this section is Golden and Durango, but both feature half a dozen or more breweries and brewpubs that you can link together into a great beer day. The options abound, but here are the favorites.

Denver River North East

Denver's River North arts district—RiNo for short—is so loaded with beer that it requires two different beer tours. Keep in mind that you can link them together, but that's a bit ambitious. Denver's mayor even declared the area the "RiNo Valley of Beer," a riff on the idea that the Front Range is the Napa Valley of beer. This crawl covers the east side of the train tracks centered on the Blake, Walnut, and Larimer streets area and features as many as 13 breweries and beer bars, so pick and choose where you want to stop.

If you want to cover this much ground, start about lunchtime at the north end at **Black Street Brewery**, **Shirt Brewing**, 3719 Walnut St., Denver, CO 80205; (303) 993-2799. The brewery makes great pizzas, so you can lay down a base layer to build endurance. Black Shirt specializes in red ales but produces a number of interesting styles. The brewery was even featured in the craft beer documentary *Crafting a Nation*. **Tip:** If you can't wait for it to open at 11 a.m., a block north is **RiNo Beer Garden**, 3800 Walnut St., Denver, CO 80205; (303) 295-3800. It opens an hour earlier on the weekends. Or if burgers are more in mind, **Oskar Blues Chuburger**, 3490 Larimer St., Denver, CO 80205; (720) 668-9167, serves 30-plus taps and good food, including doughnuts and coffee at its sister place next door, Hotbox Roasters.

From Black Shirt, walk 4 blocks south down Walnut Street to 34th Street and head west two blocks to:

River North Brewery, 3400 Blake St., Denver CO 80205; (303) 296-2617. River North left the neighborhood that gave it a name for a bit but recently returned to a new location. It's both the oldest and one of the newest in the city's beer district.

Walk two and a half blocks south on Blake Street to:

14er Brewing Company, 3120 Blake St., Denver, CO 80205; (720) 773-1437. A relative newcomer to the scene, 14er Brewing is named for the tallest mountain peaks in Colorado and offers a wide variety of beer.

Walk half a block south to 31st Street and head east one block to Walnut Street. Walk south down Walnut Street one block to:

Epic Brewing Company, 3001 Walnut St., Denver, CO 80205; (720) 539-7410. Epic is a Utah-based brewery with a second brew house in Denver, where it celebrates a massive beer list and special offerings that you can find only at the taproom. And yes, you can get a tasting flight with all of them, but you'll need friends to help. The Big Bad Baptist stout series and the RiNo APA are two favorites.

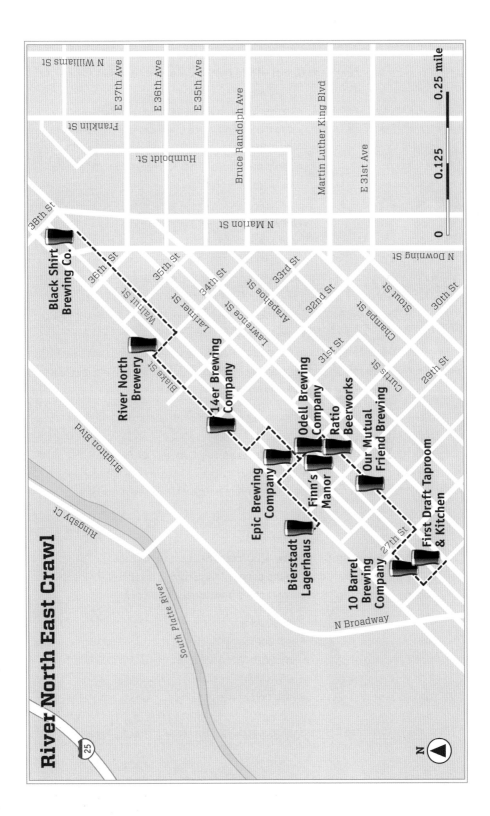

River North East Crawl

Black Shirt Brewing Co.

River North Brewery

14er Brewing Company

Epic Brewing Company

Bierstadt Lagerhaus

10 Barrel Brewing Company

Finn's Manor

Odell Brewing Company

Ratio Beerworks

Our Mutual Friend Brewing

First Draft Taproom & Kitchen

N Williams St
E 37th Ave
E 36th Ave
E 35th Ave
Bruce Randolph Ave
Martin Luther King Blvd
E 31st Ave
Franklin St
Humboldt St.
N Marion St
N Downing St

38th St
36th St
35th St
34th St
Walnut St
Larimer St
Lawrence St
Arapahoe St
Blake St
31st St
33rd St
32nd St
Champa St
Curtis St
Stout St
30th St
29th St
27th St

Brighton Blvd
Ringsby Ct
South Platte River
N Broadway

0   0.125   0.25 mile

N

25

Walk one block west back to Blake Street and head south one block to:

Bierstadt Lagerhaus, 2875 Blake St., Denver, CO 80205; (720) 570-7824. Bierstadt is located in the Rackhouse Pub and offers a good place for a snack. But the main reason to go is the Slow Pour Pils, the jewel of great German lagers in Colorado from one of the best beer makers in the nation.

Walk back toward Epic Brewing by going north one block on Blake Street and then east on 30th Avenue. Continue east on 30th Avenue until Larimer Street and turn south to:

Odell Brewing Company, 2945 Larimer St., Denver, CO 80205; (720) 795-7862. The new Denver outpost for the Fort Collins–based brewer includes its staples and a pilot brewing system that makes beers you can find only at this location.

Walk half a block south on Larimer Street to:

Finn's Manor, 2927 Larimer St., Denver, CO 80205. This beer bar proves that you don't need a gazillion taps to serve the best beer. Grab a draft from an amazing selection inside or head out back to the food truck courtyard, where a bar in a shed offers even more rare and delicious craft bottles and cans.

Walk across Larimer Street to:

Ratio Beerworks, 2920 Larimer St., Denver, CO 80205; (303) 997-8288. With so much so close, no need to rush. And Ratio is a good place to chill for a bit. Grab a seat on the outdoor patio and admire the huge mural while drinking a light Domestica and playing yard games.

Walk a block and a half south down Larimer Street to:

Our Mutual Friend Brewing Company, 2810 Larimer St., Denver, CO 80205; (303) 296-3441. The menu offers all the standbys but order one of the mixed culture saisons that the brewery is known for.

Walk a block south on Larimer Street to 27th Street. Then turn northwest one block to Walnut Street and head south to:

10 Barrel Brewing Company, 2620 Walnut St., Denver, CO 80205; (720) 573-8992. This one-time craft brewer from Portland, Oregon, is now owned by goliath Anheuser-Busch, but it makes exclusive beers on-site and offers a great food menu.

Walk half a block south to 26th Street and turn east for a short walk to:

First Draft Taproom & Kitchen, 1309 26th St., Denver, CO 80205; (303) 736-8400. At the risk of further overloading your palate, First Draft offers 30-plus taps from breweries you didn't visit. Try as many different beers and as few ounces of each as you'd like, perhaps with a few of their small plates.

Denver River North West

The city's River North beer district is divided by train tracks, so it's worth splitting into two trips. If you want, there are pedestrian bridges to cross at various points, but both sides offer great and unique beer options. There are only five main stops, all of which are pretty close together, but the tour feels long because most places will make you want to linger.

This tour can start from either direction, but if you start north and walk back toward downtown, the first stop is **Blue Moon Brewing Company**, 3750 Chestnut Place, Denver, CO 80216; (303) 728-2337. The Coors subsidiary opened a massive and beautiful tasting room and pours all sorts of made-on-site creations as well as the classics. It also serves an elevated food menu. *Tip:* Canada's **Red Truck Beer Company** also built a taproom on Brighton Boulevard if you want to make an extra stop.

Walk east on 38th Street to Delgany Street and south two blocks to:

Mockery Brewing Company, 3501 Delgany St., Denver, CO 80216; (303) 953-2058. Mockery prides itself on breaking beer conventions to make interesting brews you can't find elsewhere. The Salted Scotch Ale is a big-flavored favorite at this brewery, which is establishing itself as a Denver beer stop.

Walk one block east on 35th Street to:

Great Divide Barrel Bar, 1812 35th St., Denver, CO 80216; (303) 296-9460. The Barrel Bar is a little gem located at Great Divide's huge new brewery. It's cozy with barrel staves as a decorative motif in a room with a handful of tables and a small outdoor patio. The beer list is plentiful, so be sure to stay a while and try the Yeti stout series.

Walk half a block down Brighton Boulevard to:

Crooked Stave Artisan Beer Project, 3350 Brighton Blvd., Denver, CO 80216; (720) 550-8860. Inside The Source, a brick exterior marketplace of local vendors, you can find one of the best sour beer makers in the country. Crooked Stave has a small taproom in the back with nuanced sours and even delicious hazy IPAs. If you want food, Acorn, located in the same building, is one of the city's best restaurants.

Walk next door to:

The Woods by New Belgium Brewing Company, 3330 Brighton Blvd., Denver, CO 80216; (800) 570-6216. A rooftop level bar in The Source Hotel next door features the state's most well-known brewer, New Belgium. The Fort Collins beer maker brews exclusive small batches on the ground floor and send them to the restaurant at the top for sipping and great city views.

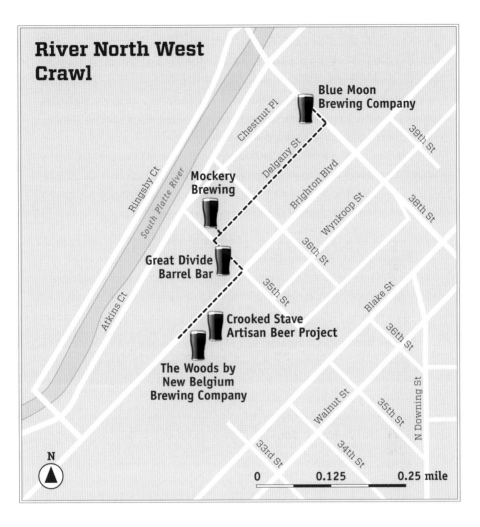

River North West Crawl

Blue Moon Brewing Company

Chestnut Pl

Delgany St

39th St

Mockery Brewing

Brighton Blvd

Wynkoop St

38th St

Great Divide Barrel Bar

36th St

35th St

Blake St

36th St

Crooked Stave Artisan Beer Project

The Woods by New Belgium Brewing Company

Walnut St

35th St

N Downing St

33rd St

34th St

Ringsby Ct

South Platte River

Atkins Ct

N

0   0.125   0.25 mile

South Denver

From downtown, Broadway stretches south with eclectic shops, restaurants, bars, clubs, and breweries. From here, you can detour to other beer places near the Santa Fe arts district, too. This path takes you to a few standouts and a few up-and-comers, so you can pick and choose how many stops to make. Take an electric scooter or ride share to cover all this ground.

Starting from downtown and heading south, a good place to eat at the start is **LowDown Brewery and Kitchen**, 800 Lincoln St., Denver, CO 80203; (720) 524-8065. The from-scratch menu makes a number of healthier options and serves pizzas alongside LowDown beers and guest taps.

Head a block west on 8th Avenue to Broadway and turn south for half a mile to:
Banded Oak Brewing Company, 3404, 470 Broadway, Denver, CO 80203; (720) 479-8033. This small brewery specializes in wine barrel–aged beers and recently won its first GABF medal for Drunkard's Cloak, a strong ale.

Walk a block and a half south on Broadway to:
Baere Brewing Company, 320 Broadway, Denver, CO 80203; (303) 733-3354. In an unassuming strip mall, Baere Brewing is making a host of interesting beers, particularly in the sour category. The IPAs are popular, too, so get a flight and try a bunch of different brews.

Cross the street at 3rd Avenue and walk half a block south on Broadway to:
TRVE Brewing Company, 227 Broadway, #101, Denver, CO 80203. The door is easy to miss, but it's there. Enter into the dark lair of heavy metal music to try great farmhouse ales from one of the city's best breweries and sit down at a long Viking table. Be sure to grab a four-pack of cans to go.

Walk a couple blocks south on Broadway to:
Historians Ale House, 24 Broadway, #102, Denver, CO 80203; (720) 479-8505. Get a beer from one of the 30-plus taps at this local's favorite and head upstairs to the rooftop deck, where you can order food and enjoy great views.

Call a ride share or cab and direct the driver south on Broadway for two miles to:
Black Project Spontaneous & Wild Ales, 1290 S. Broadway, Denver, CO 80210; (720) 900-5551. This sour-only brewery with a national following offers a revolving menu of spontaneously fermented beers. The brewer specializes in fruited beers and offers select rare bottles for purchase. ***Tip:*** A couple new breweries opened within blocks in case you want to add stops. And for craft spirits, the amazing Laws Whiskey House is a couple blocks away and offers tours by appointment.

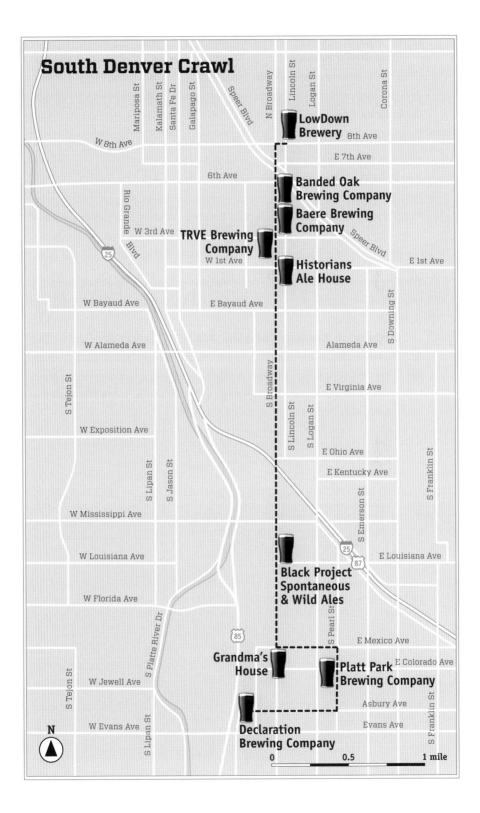

Walk or ride four blocks south on Broadway to:

Grandma's House, 1710 S. Broadway, Denver, CO 80210; (303) 578-6754. This brewery is possibly the most unusual you will find in Denver. It tries to evoke the feeling of a grandmother's house with knitting themes and vintage video games.

Optional: Take a detour from Broadway and head east on Mexico Avenue six blocks to South Pearl Street, then turn south two blocks to:

Platt Park Brewing Company, 1875 S. Pearl St., Denver, CO 80210; (303) 993-4002. On a quaint street with shops, coffee houses, and restaurants, Platt Park Brewing is the neighborhood brewery. It makes a range of styles and opens its doors to the street in warm weather. A great ice cream shop and a burger restaurant are across the street.

Whether you kept walking south or detoured into South Pearl Street, find your way to East Asbury Avenue and head west from Broadway to South Cherokee Street to:

Declaration Brewing Company, 2030 S. Cherokee St., Denver, CO 80223; (303) 955-7410. Located in an industrial warehouse park tucked along the railroad tracks, Declaration offers a long menu of beers and a great atmosphere with yard games, ping-pong, and food trucks. It's not far from the Evans light-rail station to help you find a way home.

Downtown Denver

`The combination of proximity and public transportation makes downtown Denver an easy place for a lengthy beer crawl. The problem is figuring out where to start and finish and which stops to make in between. This tour includes about a dozen options to help you design a custom trip.

If you want to end up downtown, the best place to start is just outside the city center at the must-visit **Goed Zuur**, 2801 Welton St., Denver, CO 80205; (720) 749-2709. The place claims itself as the world's first sour-only beer bar and serves some of the rarest and most interesting brews from around the globe.

Cross the street and walk half a block south on Welton Street to:

Spangalang Brewery, 2736 Welton St., Denver, CO 80205; (303) 297-1276. A hidden locals' favorite, Spangalang was founded by former Great Divide brewers who wanted more creative freedom. The tap list shows the creativity with subtle Belgians and powerful IPAs and stouts.

Walk or scooter about half a mile west on 27th Street and south down Champa Street to find:

Liberati Osteria & Oenobeers, 2403 Champa St., Denver, CO 80205; (303) 862-5652. It's not far from the beaten path, but the flavors here sure will seem foreign. Liberati specializes in wine-beer hybrid beers and pairs them with Italian food in this beautiful taproom.

Walk two blocks east on 24th Street and two blocks south on California Street to:

Woods Boss Brewing Company, 2210 California St., Denver, CO 80205; (720) 642-7177. Another good stop between the start and downtown, Woods Boss makes all styles of beer and serves them in a taproom with forest tones, high ceilings, and great light.

Walk or scooter the remaining four blocks toward downtown by taking 22nd Street northwest to:

Great Divide Brewing Company, 2201 Arapahoe St., Denver, CO 80205; (303) 296-9460. The brewery's original location downtown still makes beer here. The small taproom is a great place for a hallmark Denver brew and a glimpse of the brewing operations.

Walk two blocks south on Arapahoe Street and one block north on 20th Street to:

Jagged Mountain Craft Brewery, 139 20th St., Denver, CO 80202; (720) 689-2337. The brewery offers an ambitious menu of quirky styles and barrel-aged options.

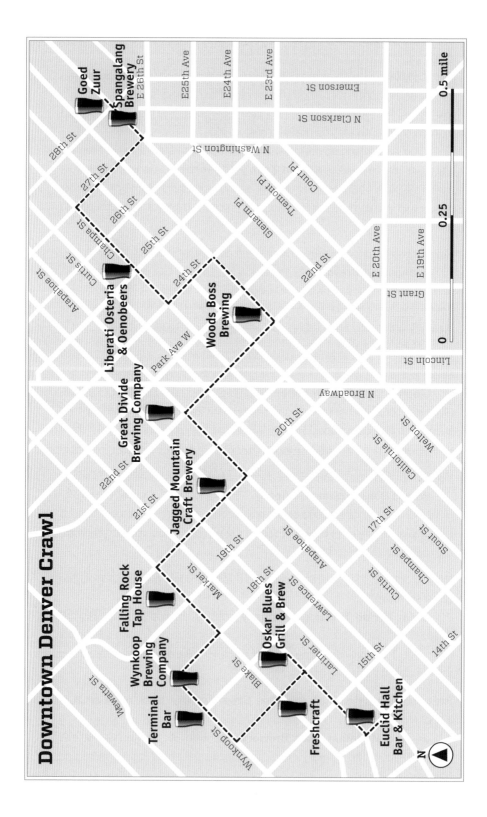

Downtown Denver Crawl

Walk three blocks northwest on 20th Avenue and one block south on Blake Street to:

Falling Rock Tap House, 1919 Blake St., Denver, CO 80202; (303) 293-8338. Pace yourself before you get here so you can buy multiple pints from the 70 taps and extensive bottle list featuring some of the nation's and Colorado's best beers.

Walk a block south on Blake Street and two blocks west on 18th Street to:

Wynkoop Brewing Company, 1634 18th St., Denver, CO 80202; (303) 297-2700. The state's original brewpub keeps a fresh menu of new styles, including barrel-aged and sour beers, as well as the mainstays. The menu offer great pub food, too.

Walk one block south on Wynkoop Street to:

Terminal Bar, 1701 Wynkoop St., Denver, CO 80211; (720) 460-3701. Inside Union Station, at the old ticket window, you can now find 30 taps of Colorado beers and one of the most unique drinking experiences in the state. Grab a beer and a seat in the terminal to sip and watch as travelers pass by.

Walk a block south to 16th Street and grab the free pedestrian mall bus east. Exit at Blake Street and walk half a block south to:

Freshcraft, 1530 Blake St., Denver, CO 80202; (303) 758-9608. A great selection of craft beer, an extensive bottle list, and a comfort-food menu merit a pit stop.

Head back to 16th Street and one block east to Market Street. Walk half a block to:

Oskar Blues Grill & Brew, 1624 Market St., Denver, CO 80202; (720) 502-3535. The Longmont brewer's restaurants offer all its flagship beers and those from its Canarchy collective of other breweries from across the nation. Downstairs, you'll find a live music venue.

Walk two blocks south on Market Street, then half a block east on 14th Street to:

Euclid Hall Bar & Kitchen, 1317 14th St., Denver, CO 80202; (303) 595-4255. Even with all the food options on this tour, save an appetite for Euclid Hall, an upscale pub that serves great beers in a casual setting. **Tip:** If it's summer, continue the tour by walking around the corner through the picturesque Larimer Square to the 16th Street pedestrian mall and east to the corner of Arapahoe Street. Here you can find a beer garden with yard games and fun in the middle of downtown Denver.

Boulder

The Boulder beer tour requires advanced planning. The breweries and beer bars are concentrated in little clusters each a distance from another. This pub crawl focuses on the core of the college town and offers two options to extend the tour.

Start downtown at **The West End Tavern**, 926 Pearl St., Boulder, CO 80302; (303) 444-3535. And start with food from the great menu while you select a beer from the curated tap and bottle list.

Walk across the street to:

Oskar Blues Boulder Taproom, 921 Pearl St., Boulder, CO 80302; (720) 645-1749. The Longmont brewer offers an extensive tap list of its core beers and those from its brewery partners as well as classic pub food.

Walk east on Pearl Street until it turns into a pedestrian mall to:

West Flanders Brewing Company, 1125 Pearl St., Boulder, CO 80302; (303) 447-2739. The only brewery on the much-visited pedestrian mall is a Belgian-inspired brewpub that makes creative small batches.

Walk east to Broadway and south two blocks to:

Rueben's Burger Bistro, 1800 Broadway, Boulder CO 80302; (303) 443-5000. The 40 rotating taps and a lengthy bottle list pair well with a huge burger menu and design-your-own mac and cheese.

Walk back to the Pearl Street pedestrian mall and east four blocks to:

Mountain Sun Pub & Brewery, 1535 Pearl St., Boulder, CO 80302; (303) 546-0886. The hippie vibe at Mountain Sun will capture Boulder in a single spot. The house beers are great, and the food is fresh and seasonal.

Walk 15 minutes, heading four blocks south on 16th Street and seven blocks east on Arapahoe Avenue to:

Backcountry Pizza & Tap House, 2319 Arapahoe Ave., Boulder, CO 80302; (303) 449-4285. One of the best beer bars in America, Backcountry's huge selection of American craft and imported beer hits all the highlights. The pizzas are a good pick, too.

Here's where you can go multiple directions because it requires a lengthy walk, a bike, or a ride share to visit the remaining breweries.

Option 1: East Boulder

Get a ride or walk the mile east on Arapahoe Avenue to:

Fate Brewing Company, 1600 38th St., Boulder, CO 80301; (303) 449-3283. This brewpub offers craft beers and eats. The 30-rotating taps offer a wide array of house brews and guest pints.

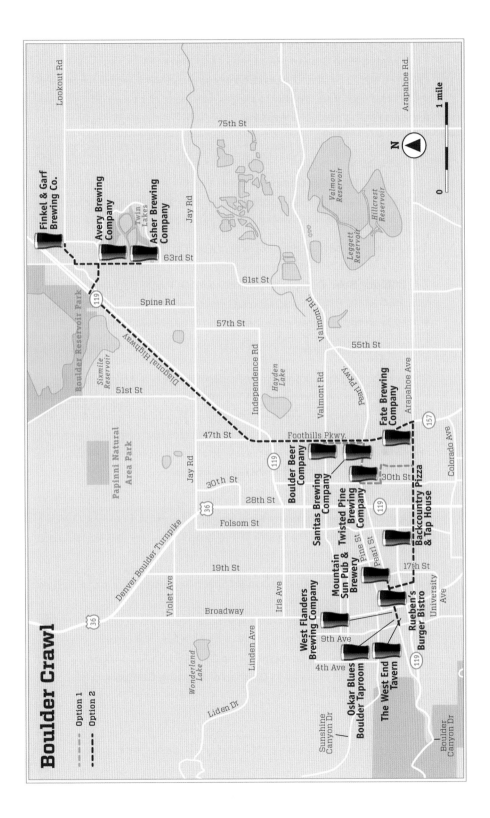

Get a ride or walk another mile north on 33rd Street to Walnut Street to:

Twisted Pine Brewing Company, 3201 Walnut St., Boulder, CO 80301; (303) 786-9270. Twisted Pine pours a lot of special beers in addition to its year-rounds and seasonals. Be sure to sample its famous chili beers, Billy's Chilies, and the extra-hot Ghost Face Killah.

Get a ride north on 30th and east on Pearl Parkway or cut across the train tracks behind the climbing gym to:

Sanitas Brewing Company, 3550 Frontier Ave., Boulder, CO 80301; (303) 442-4130. A great deck with a built-in taco truck along the train tracks makes this a perfect outdoor spot to hang with a beer.

Take the walking path on the west side of Foothills Parkway, then west on the Goose Creek Path and up Wilderness Place to:

Boulder Beer Company, 2880 Wilderness Place, Boulder, CO 80301; (303) 444-8448. This is the oldest craft brewery in Colorado, and a trip here to enjoy a fresh pint of Hazed is an absolute rite of passage and a treat.

Option 2: North Boulder

Whether you start from downtown or Boulder Beer, take a ride share north to:

Avery Brewing Company, 4910 Nautilus Ct. N, Boulder, CO 80301; (303) 440-4324. The massive new Avery brew house is outside the downtown core but worth the journey. The temple to beer offers great taproom-only selections, along with the core brews, and a catwalk tour over the brewing operation. The food menu and outdoor seating are big draws, too.

Walk a short distance down Nautilus Court to:

Asher Brewing Company, 4699 Nautilus Ct. S, #104, Boulder, CO 80301; 303-530-1381. Asher is the state's first all-organic brewery and specializes in IPAs.

Get a ride or walk one mile north on 63rd Street, then east on Lookout Road and up Spine Road and loop around to:

Finkel & Garf Brewing Company, 5455 Spine Rd., Boulder, CO 80301; (720) 379-6042. Founded by a father-and-son team, the brewery offers the standard styles in a nice taproom. Try the Oatmeal Milk Stout. ***Tip:*** If you want to keep going, find your way to **Gunbarrel Brewing Company** a mile or so away.

Fort Collins

A bike is the best way to tour Fort Collins beer spots. You can bring your own, hire a tour company, or join the bike share in town. After all, the city is home to bike-inspired New Belgium Brewing and its Fat Tire amber ale. This tour hits the breweries and returns downtown to great beer bars. ***Tip:*** On the way into town, visit **Jessup Farm Barrel House** or **Purpose Brewing & Cellars**.

Starting near the corner of Mason Street and Laporte Avenue downtown, near a bike share dock, head east on Walnut Street and then turn north on Linden Street a few blocks to:

New Belgium Brewing Company, 500 Linden St., Fort Collins, CO 80524; (970) 221-0524. New Belgium is one of the largest craft breweries in America and the best known in Colorado. Book a free tour well in advance or grab one of the brewery-only beers inside and return to the front yard to lounge under an umbrella or play yard games.

Bike back south toward town on Linden Street and take the Poudre Trail biking path on the left to East Lincoln Avenue. Turn east and bike down Lincoln to:

Odell Brewing Company, 800 E. Lincoln Ave., Fort Collins, CO 80524; (970) 498-9070. The taproom here pours a dizzying number of year-rounds, seasonals, and special releases. Try an Odell IPA, a Colorado icon, and then sample from the list of pilot brews.

Continue east on East Lincoln Avenue a short distance and head north at 9th Street to:

Snowbank Brewing, 225 N. Lemay Ave., Suite 1, Fort Collins, CO 80524; (970) 999-5658. This small brewery appeals to a range of beer tastes. But try the Cranknbrew, a coffee pale ale. ***Tip:*** On the way, you passed **Red Truck Beer Company**, a Canadian brewer with a range of beers, in case you want to add a stop.

Head back to East Lincoln Avenue and continue east for 0.7 miles. Turn left on Commerce Drive and go until it ends at Racquette Drive. Make a right to:

Horse & Dragon Brewing Company, 124 Racquette Dr., Fort Collins, CO 80524; (970) 631-8038. Tucked back in an industrial park, Horse & Dragon makes a great list of interesting ales. Order the Sad Panda Coffee Stout.

Return to East Lincoln Avenue and head east a couple blocks to:

Funkwerks, 1900 E. Lincoln Ave., Unit B, Fort Collins, CO 80524; (970) 482-3865. This is the place to indulge in saisons and sours with nuance and great flavor. Be sure to taste the barrel-room reserve series.

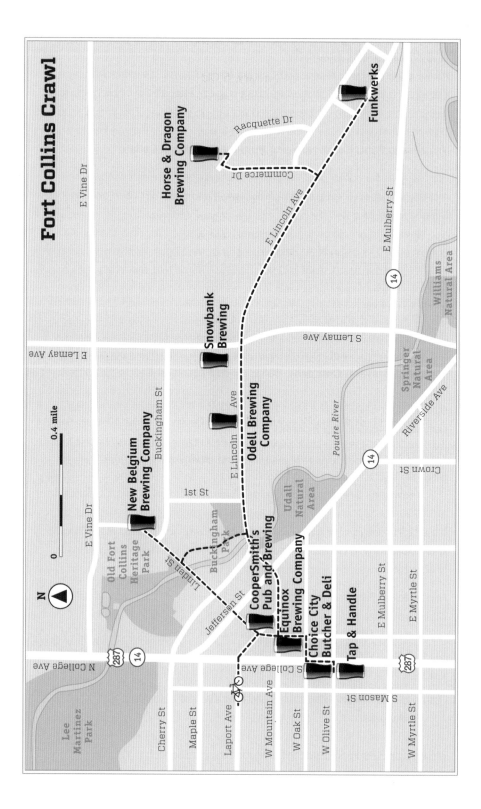

Turn back toward town, taking East Lincoln Avenue and then East Mountain Avenue west for two miles to:

CooperSmith's Pub and Brewery, 5 Old Town Sq., Fort Collins, CO 80524; (970) 498-0483. Now that you are back downtown, you can return or park the bike and walk the remainder of the tour. CooperSmith's is a traditional brewpub with a hearty menu. The number of different house-brewed beers also is impressive.

Walk across the street and head south on Remington Street half a block to:

Equinox Brewing Company, 133 Remington St., Fort Collins, CO 80524; (970) 484-1368. Even at this point in the tour, Equinox is sure to have a beer you haven't tried. Take it to the courtyard if the weather is nice.

Walk a block south on Remington Street and turn down the pedestrian path opposite East Oak Street and walk west to South College Avenue. Head south a block and a half to:

Choice City Butcher & Deli, 104 W. Olive St., Fort Collins, CO 80524; (970) 490-2489. Another good place for a quick bite to eat. The 40 taps behind the bar pour some of the rarest beers you'll find in the state, and there is a nice list of bottles.

Cross West Olive Street and walk south on South College Avenue half a block to:

Tap and Handle, 307 S. College Ave., Fort Collins, CO 80524; (970) 484-1116. A visit to one of the best beer bars in America is a great way to end the tour. Find plenty of special-release beers and others to satisfy whatever style you missed along the way.

Beer Lover's Pick List

Barrel Aged Yeti, Great Divide Brewing Company, Barrel-Aged Imperial Stout

Black IPA, Sanitas Brewing Company, Black IPA

Bligh's Barleywine Ale, Dry Dock Brewing Company, English Barleywine

Blue Moon Belgian White Ale, Blue Moon Brewing Company, Belgian Witbier

'Bout Damn Time, Four Noses Brewing Company, American IPA

Brush Creek Blonde, Bonfire Brewing, American Blonde Ale

Codename: Superfan, Odd13 Brewing, Hazy IPA

Colorado Kölsch, Steamworks Brewing Company, Kölsch-Style Ale

Coors Banquet, Coors Brewing Company/AC Golden (MillerCoors), American-Style Lager

Dreamy Thing, Cerebral Brewing Company, Brett Saison

Dyad, New Image Brewing, Brett Saison

8 Second Kölsch, Elevation Beer Company, Kölsch-Style Ale

Fade to Black, Vol. 1, Left Hand Brewing Company, Foreign Export Stout

Genius Wizard, Ratio Beerworks, Whiskey Barrel–Aged Imperial Stout

Ghost Face Killah, Twisted Pine Brewing Company, Chili Beer

Graham Cracker Porter, Denver Beer Company/Cerveceria Colorado, Porter

Greensky American Lager, Telluride Brewing Company, American Lager

In the Steep, Outer Range Brewing Company, Hazy IPA

IPA, Odell Brewing Company, IPA

Johnson's Farm, Phantom Canyon Brewing Company, Kettle Sour

Juicy Bits, WeldWerks Brewing Company, New England–Style IPA

Killer Penguin, Boulder Beer Company, American Barleywine

La Folie, New Belgium Brewing Company, Flanders-Style Sour Brown Ale

Laughing Lab Scottish Ale, Bristol Brewing Company, Scottish Ale

Oktoberfest, Ska Brewing Company, German-Style Lager

Old Jubilation Ale, Avery Brewing Company, Old Ale

Peach Casey Family Preserves, Casey Brewing & Blending, Saison

Persica, Crooked Stave Artisan Beer Project, Golden Sour Ale

Pinner Throwback IPA, Oskar Blues Brewery, Session IPA

Red Swingline, Trinity Brewing Company, Sour IPA

Rocky Mountain Oyster Stout, Wynkoop Brewing Company, Foreign Export Stout

Roswell, Black Project Spontaneous & Wild Ales, Lambic Inspired

Sad Panda, Horse & Dragon Brewing Company, Coffee Stout

Serenity Now, Storm Peak Brewing Company, Kettle Sour

Slow Pour Pils, Bierstadt Lagerhaus, Northern German Pilsner

Superpower, Comrade Brewing Company, IPA

Tangerine Cream, Station 26 Brewing Company, Cream Ale

Tropic King, Funkwerks, Imperial Saison

Vanilla Caramel Amber, Lone Tree Brewing Company, Amber Ale

A decade or so ago, when I had a beer awakening, I never imagined it would lead to this book. As a journalist, I imagined possibly writing a book, but not about beer. So now that it's done, I'm reflecting on how I came to this point—how I tasted thousands of beers, visited hundreds of breweries, sat through hours of sensory training, judged numerous competitions, made countless batches of homebrew, and wrote dozens upon dozens of published stories about a single beverage made with four simple ingredients.

The journey from awareness to passion did not occur alone. I owe most everything, in beer and life, to my amazing wife, Kate. She bought the first craft beer that blew my mind, a four-pack of Oskar Blues Gubna Imperial IPA, and joined me on a path of constant education and discovery. Along the way, she became a beer expert herself. In fact, a North Carolina brewery executive, who wisely realized she is the secret force behind all my work, dubbed her Mrs. Beer Writer. Her patience for vacation detours to breweries and long lines at bottle releases is unexplainable. Her encouragement and understanding for all the weekends spent writing this book and dozens of beer stories, which often didn't fall under my official job title or pay enough to justify the time, is remarkable. And this doesn't even include her tolerance for all the homebrewing disasters through the years. Because I don't say it enough, thank you, Kate. A similarly special thanks to Lucy, our furry four-legged companion whose favorite beers are stouts and who helped this project stay on course by lying so close behind my desk chair that I couldn't take writing breaks.

I can't imagine completing the book if author Lee Williams didn't outline the path with the first edition of *Beer Lover's Colorado* in 2012. I'm honored to take the mantle. A thank you to my editors at Globe Pequot Press, whose call led me into this arduous but fulfilling project. And an extra thanks to photographer Dustin Hall at The Brewtography Project, whose stunning images fill this book. His best work is found in his own book, *Discovering Colorado Breweries*, so go buy one.

A handful of other people selflessly contributed to this book in immeasurable ways without getting their name on the front cover. These are Colorado's talented and passionate cohort of beer writers, all of whom acted as a sounding board and helped pick the breweries featured—Jonathan Shikes at *Westword*, Ed Sealover at the *Denver Business Journal*, Tristan Chan at PorchDrinking .com, Eric Gorski and Jeremy Meyer formerly of the *Denver Post*, and Ryan

Hannigan at Focus on the Beer. And be sure to check out Ed's great book, *Colorado Excursions with History, Hikes and Hops*.

The brewers, bar owners, and festival organizers who took time to tell me about their fine establishments deserve most the credit. It's much easier to write about beer than make it, trust me. A special shout-out goes to: Alexandra Weissner, the founder of Lexa PR, and Emily Tracy; Chea Franz and Emily Hutto from RadCraft; Ann Obenchain at the Brewers Association; and Abby Hagstrom at ALH Communications. Steve Kurowski, formerly of the Colorado Brewers Guild, is another indispensable resource for all things beer.

So many other people deserve credit for helping me get to this point. The real-life beer experts who make me smarter, Neil Fisher, Nicole Garneau, Julia Herz, John Holl, and so many more. Additional appreciation to the friends who meet at breweries without a protest and share their own great beer, Will Chesser, Foster Ramsey, Jon Murray, Daniel Bruning, Jenn Fields, J. D. Schlick, and Jon Macklin. Also, Brendan Watson and Alex Miller, thank you for teaching me how to brew long ago. The same to my supportive parents as well as my brothers, Scott and Erik, who share my passion and their beer. And not least, my colleagues at the *Colorado Sun*, who didn't complain when I agreed to write a book at the same time we started a revolutionary new online journalism enterprise in Colorado. Thanks to all for helping make this possible. And keep reading more Colorado beer dispatches from me at coloradosun.com.

John Frank is a beer columnist and political reporter at the *Colorado Sun* and formerly of the *Denver Post*. He has written about beer for seven years, and his work also has appeared in *All About Beer* magazine. When he's not writing, he's traveling for a good pint or brewing his own beer at his home in Denver, Colorado.

Dustin Hall is the author of *Discovering Colorado Breweries*, a 232-page coffee table book published in 2018 with the help of his wife, Marcia. The book, which started as a Kickstarter project, features behind-the-scenes photographs from more than 70 Colorado craft breweries.

An avid photographer and homebrewer, Dustin combined his passions to document the unique personality, feel, and methodology at different breweries. The project's goal was to tell the stories of Colorado breweries and the people who work there, providing a window into the culture of the industry.

Dustin continues to photograph breweries and beer events and documents his work at brewtographyproject.com. He lives in Denver, Colorado.

David Sands